Mummy:
A Journey Home

by

Darren Timothy Numer

Steel Star Publishing

This is a memoir. Actual events are depicted, as recalled to the best of the author's ability. Many people's actual names, physical descriptions and details have been changed in an effort to protect anonymity.

Like **Darren Numer** on Facebook to keep up with news and information about upcoming personal appearances, book signings and other events. And follow **@DagwoodLA** on Instagram.

Numer, Darren Timothy
Mummy: A Journey Home

ISBN: 978-1-7323409-0-9

Printed in the U.S.A.
First American edition, August 2018

Acknowledgments

I would like to make two acknowledgements. And that would be to my editor, Rita M. Reali, and my graphic designer, Al Esper, whom Rita introduced me to. Rita and I became friends first on Facebook. I was online, bragging about my wanting to write my life story within 90 days. She was bragging about a cake she made for her husband. I complimented her on her cake looking so awesome. And she in return encouraged me in my writing and mentioned she was an author herself, and an editor. After a few back-and-forth comments, we exchanged phone numbers and the rest, as they say, is history. Then, in addition to all this excitement, Al Esper, now *our* graphic designer, after only one conversation, three days later presented me with this amazing book cover. In one swing, he knocked it out the park. Too awesome!

Thank you, Universe.

Dedication

I have three parties I would like to dedicate this book to. And I want to put them in backwards from the order I met them in.

I'll start with my Crenshaw Rotary Club. I've been with them close to a year now and am still in awe they invited me into their club. This organization is ferociously dedicated to helping children, veterans and others who are in need of a helping hand in their journey of life. Whether it would be through a Thanksgiving box full of food, or through a gift of dictionaries for students who may not have one. You see, I was one of those people who received a meal when I was hungry. And I was given a dictionary when I couldn't spell. So to see this full circle in my life just blows my mind. Thank you, Crenshaw Rotary.

Dear Los Angeles, I Love you. And I want to protect you. So I'm gonna put it the only way I'm used to. Yes, we have the worst weather on the whole planet, with your earthquakes on the hour every hour. Torrential rainstorms every single morning, like clockwork. Riots on every single street corner. But even with all that, I Love you. I really do.

To my husband, just as the same as the last two parties I mentioned. The moment I met all of you, I grew two feet taller. And for that, I dedicate this book to you.

Mummy:
A Journey Home

Darren Timothy Numer

No More Running Away

Oh, God, where do I begin…?

This is my story. I'm a 47-year-old man sitting at a computer, slowly trying to pick apart and sift through the memories flooding my brain… terrified of the truths I know, but not so scared that I'm going to run away. I don't run away anymore, but there was definitely a time when running away was the best choice I could make in my life. That's not an option anymore.

Let me start by saying I can't believe I'm alive and not rotting in some corner of a padded room, rocking back and forth in a fetal position, thumb in mouth. That was never really me to begin with. I remember being a happy child. And whenever I wasn't happy, I would go hide. I'd hide under the bed, in the coat closet, down in the dark, cold basement; I'd even hide behind the mailbox down the street.

Earliest Memories

My earliest memories are only split-second thoughts. I remember when I was 2 or 3 years old, we lived in a two-story house with a curved staircase my two older brothers, Billy and Ricky, and my sister, Lisa, would slide down on flattened cardboard boxes. To this day I can still hear our uncontrollable laughter and glee. At that same age, I remember getting cut, right above my inner right ankle, by a broken Pepsi bottle I fell on. I'd stare at that scar all my young foster-childhood life, begging God to return me to that time and that bottle, which never happened. My biological mother, Mummy, said I loved to run around naked all day long; and if I wore anything, it was a fur coat, nothing else.

We lived in the town of Garfield on the North Side of Pittsburgh, Pennsylvania. We were so poor that when we went on vacation it was really only a visit behind the house to the local cemetery. We would pack a blanket and a brown paper bag containing Mummy's beer. Mummy liked her beer, or so I was told. I was also told we were the only white people on our block. I commend Mummy for that, because she was by herself with four children and slowly losing her mind. I didn't know this at the time, but life would show this to me eventually. I believe my siblings and I all had different fathers. Billy's dad was William Penman Numer II. He may have been Ricky's dad, too, but I never knew for sure.

I do remember being introduced to William II as a

teenager by my eldest brother, Billy, on a rare visit to his house when I was 13. It was at his biological grandmother's gorgeous three-story wood-trimmed maroon-and-brown Victorian home. This whole house was all for only Billy and Grandma Numer! Technically, because the rest of us rugrats weren't Numers, biologically, our presence was not welcome. Billy and his dad were outside recementing the sidewalk, or something like that. Billy hollered to me to come meet his dad – and boy, did he look like Ricky!

I shook his hand, said hello, then scurried back into the house and hid behind the screen door to spy on them. Every time I heard Billy call him Dad, my head lowered with jealousy and sadness.

Now, Lisa's dad, if I'm correct, was named Snake. That's all I've got on that. If it's true, I guess today his name would be Grandpa Snake. As for my dad, I'm blessed to know at least a little about him. Mummy told me our landlord's young-adult son came to the house one afternoon with a bottle of wine. Then after a few drinks came the good times, if you get my meaning. Please understand, Mummy was beautiful, y'all. Elizabeth Taylor beautiful, and you know how heterosexual guys get around hot chicks.

Then nine months later, ta da! A star was born – me. Through the grapevine Mummy heard Timothy McNulty (a.k.a. Dad) became a successful doctor and moved to California. I wonder if, deep down, that's why I ended up in California. Nahhh, I'm a damn good entertainer that's why.

Mummy's Last Straw

What comes next is from my brother's perspective; I truly have no memory of it. Nor does my sister – and, from what I've heard, that's a good thing.

My brothers told me how Mummy once came home and spray painted a huge swastika on the living-room wall with black paint. I don't know why, nor did I ever have the balls to ask her about it. I'm assuming it may have been the beginning stages of schizophrenia. I was also told (and this always makes me laugh for some reason) when Mummy was like seven months pregnant with me, she fell out our second-story window while trying to clean them; that may have had something to do with her issues.

At any rate, my sister Lisa was the hardest door knocker of us all. My brothers told me Mummy smacked her hard a bunch of times, just for being herself. This fact wouldn't enter my consciousness 'til I was in my late 30s. I'm a year younger than Lisa, so I ought to have some memories of us together as toddlers, but I don't, really.

However, it would be Lisa's penchant for getting smacked that would rescue us from Mummy's spiraling south demise. Only, this time, Lisa's beat down wasn't from Mummy. No, this time it came from a neighbor. Big mistake, neighbor.

Lisa came home crying, reporting her injuries into the mothering arms of the one who at any other time would have been doing the smacking.

I'm convinced that at that moment the last walnut

in Mummy's head must have cracked. The realization struck that the pain her daughter had endured so many times before was due to the "man in the mirror" staring back.

Then, *ding!-ding!-ding!* out came da gloves.

"Ahh, hell no! You ain't gonna touch *my* child!" must have been what Mummy was thinking when she pulled Lisa's offender out of her home – and didn't let off her 'til the police arrived to pry her away from that neighbor.

Mummy got arrested for the last time in front of us. I remember we got put into the back of some stranger's car. I stood up, looking out the back window. I was like, "Bye guys, we'll be right back; we're just going to the store." It was a bright, sunny afternoon. We never went back... never.

Years later, Ricky told me, they tore down the whole block. So we couldn't have gone back there if we wanted to.

Welcome to Shelter Living

That same afternoon, we ended up at the McIntyre Shelter Orphanage – which I learned much later was rumored to have been owned by the Mafia. Today it's the Ross Park Mall, in Ross Township. But back then it was my new home. This was a shelter with 10 large, separate two-story rectangular buildings they called "cottages." Cement-block buildings painted lima-bean green. Each cottage housed children of different ages. Cottage One was the main office, where every child was brought in, evaluated and then, according to their age, sent off to the appropriate cottage. The property must have been at least five acres. The landscape was set up in a kidney shape on top of a great big hill. The cottages were set across from each other. Cottages 3, 5, 7 and 9 – the boys' cottages – were on one side. Cottages 2, 4, 6, 8 and 10, on the other side, were the girls' cottages. So, making an educated guess, as the youngest in our group, I must have been sent to Cottage 3, for the babies and toddlers. Lisa had to have been sent to Cottage 2. Ricky and Billy must have been put in Cottage 5.

I do have one memory of this stay at the kiddies' slammer hotel. I was still 3 years old. It was night time; about 10 little kids and I were standing naked in the hallway on the second floor. It was shower time and we were waiting our turn to get washed. I kind of remember the kid in front of me turning around and touching my ding-a-ling. So naturally I grabbed the ding-a-ling of the kid behind me.

The second I did, he hollered out, "Mrs. Smith, Darren squeezed my thingy!" and then he started crying.

I remember looking at him like, *Settle down, you touched me first! Oh wait, you never even touched me! Damn sorry, kid.* It was fun for a while. I can still see in slow motion. Mrs. Smith, a short old white lady with wiry red hair, got right into my face. She was really pissed!

"What's wrong with you? Do you think that's nice? Well, do you? How would you like it if someone did that to you?"

Before I could answer any of her four questions, she cranked down on my penis with the strength of a lock-jaw piranha, nails and all.

"How do you like that?!" she asked.

My tears answered for me.

I cried through the hallway, in the shower, and then on my pillow 'til I fell asleep. After that, I have no memory of the next year or more of my childhood.

Foster Care, Take One

When I was 4 or 5, I was given to a foster family who lived on a dead-end road. The house was a red brick split-level home. A mom, a dad and two children already lived there. I never knew whether the kids were theirs or foster kids like me. I'm inclined to think they were theirs. I did know the kids didn't like me, but I don't want to get too ahead of myself.

I can't recall the name of the caseworker assigned to me, but she was sweet and wholesome, a nice lady – right out of an episode of *Little House on the Prairie* nice. She knelt down in front of me and fixed the collar on my yellow-, red- and blue-checkered polyester suit. She straightened my tie, then licked her fingers and slicked back the cowlick at the back of my head.

"These nice people are going to take good care of you, Darren," she said. "So you be good, okay? Now give me a big hug good bye."

Then off she went, out the door. I was left with the woman and her two kids in their living room. The dad would not be home 'til 6 for dinner. I remember watching the mom staring out the window behind her sheer curtains.

She was watching long and hard, so I got to take in all her beauty. She looked just like Cher, back when Sonny and Cher were first together. Long, beautiful jet-black hair that hung down past her butt. Her two kids went running off somewhere. I remained still, watching this woman. She was wearing a long silky pink robe.

A split second later, my new foster mom turned her eyes right at me. "Well, she's gone." She pulled her robe open, revealing not one stitch of clothing underneath.

Dropping the robe to the floor, she said, "Come on, Darren, let's go into the kitchen and get you something to eat. You must be hungry. Are you hungry?"

I spent less than a year with this foster family and I blocked out much of my time there. What I do remember is that the brother and sister duo would lock me in the basement and turn the lights out, all the time. One good memory I do have of those wonderful basement stays (too bad there's no sarcasm font!) is the time I came across a transistor radio with an earpiece, which was awesome. I would have to hide it, though, because if they knew I was able to stop the fear of the dark basement by listening to a baseball game on the radio, they surely would have taken it from me! I also remember the other kids used to call me rabbit, because during breakfast, they wouldn't share their Trix cereal with me. They'd say, "Silly rabbit, Trix are for kids, not rabbits." God, those kids were mean!

Then the dad… oh boy, just like the mom, he enjoyed being naked! He would always set me on his lap, forcefully, in the living room while sitting in that oversized brown sofa chair. I tried to squirm away, but he pulled me closer, right on top of his junk.

The mom would yell out from the other room, "Come on, Dad, stop that!"

And he'd always reply with that shitty giggle of his, "What?" trying to sound all innocent.

I do remember him placing me in the middle of the bed in the master bedroom once or twice, then he closed the door behind us. I remember this clearly because their bedroom was strictly off limits always, so I found it a treat to be allowed in there at all. I'd love to say he just let me sleep there. Yeah, right. I do remember being really tired, and that's all I remember.

Months later I would be pulled out of that home so fast, and I don't think it was for a good reason. I was sent back to McIntyre Shelter. I don't remember, but I'm sure I must have been scared as hell having to return to that piranha-pinching bitch.

The next thing I recall was when I was 6.

Foster Care, Take Two...
Home Sweet Home!

New day, new county caseworker and new foster-family audition. The potential foster mother and father met us out front of their two-story red brick house. It had a white aluminum awning over the front porch and a curved side-walk leading from the driveway to the front door. They had huge smiles on their faces... and as they greeted me, a rainbow formed over the town. I'm just kidding, but it kind of did have that feel.

My caseworker said, "Darren, this is Mr. and Mrs. Heart. They're going to let you stay for the weekend and, if you'd like, you can stay forever with them."

My first meal with the Hearts that afternoon was spaghetti and meatballs, with bread and butter and a big glass of milk.

Mr. Heart taught me how to twirl the spaghetti on a spoon. That was awesome! He cared and it showed. Mrs. Heart was nice, too; not very talkative toward me, but nice.

The weekend went so fast I don't recall too much. I do remember being in the backyard, at the end of the black tar driveway, hiding behind my new foster father's legs as he tried to introduce me to a few of the neighbor kids who wanted to meet me. But I wasn't ready and ran into the house, petrified. I can still hear the foster dad apologizing on behalf of my shyness.

Another memory was the following Monday. Around noontime my county caseworker came by and said if I wanted to stay I could – and not have to go back to that hellafied shelter. Just like that, I had a new home!

I was in awe of this house. It had a living room with a huge seven-foot-high by 10-foot-wide wall mirror… a large floor stereo, two cushioned chairs facing the large color TV… a big couch in front of the mirror and a living-room table, with an ashtray stand right next to one of the chairs, and these huge, thick, light-yellow curtains on the windows at opposite sides of the room.

A staircase separated the Hearts' living room from the dining room with its enormous dining-room table and surrounding chairs. Through the dining room was a cute, fully applianced little yellow kitchen, three chairs and a breakfast table beside two open swinging windows that looked out over the spacious backyard. The backyard hosted a large oak tree, and under it were two full-size cement lawn-décor deer.

In the kitchen, if you made a hard right it would lead you to a door that led down to the basement. You better know it was a good while 'til I ever went down there! Upstairs were two bedrooms, a sewing room and a washroom with a tub and a shower curtain. Finally, home sweet home!

The Hearts literally saved me.

But what comes after a new beautiful home and good food? Time to learn, at school. I remember being brought to the Highland Grade School and introduced to my first-grade teacher. She was tall and quarterback big, with short golden wavy hair and blue eyes. I liked looking at her, she was uniquely pretty, until we locked eyes. Then she turned into the Hulk with a twitch in her eye, and then I'd get scared with nowhere to hide.

When my foster mom left, I was seated front row far right, almost next to the teacher's desk. She started handing out our letter-learning lesson. Mind you, the school term had begun a few weeks earlier. So I'm late to the plate already.

Today's assignment is drawing the letter O.

Oh my God, this is hard! I mean like what-the-hell! hard. Lady teacher, are you telling me I have to make my usual straight pencil line (that I'm damn good at, by the way) and have to now turn it into a circle? Are you kidding me?!

I looked around at the other kids' progress. Boy, was that a wrong move!

"Darren!" the teacher yelled out. "Eyes on your own paper!"

I obeyed her command and proceeded to draw five of the squiggliest letter Os you ever did see. So that was the assignment and I was finished first out of 20 classmates. Then, from the corner of my eye to the left, I noticed a boy with his arm up, as if in panic mode.

Our teacher noticed him, too. "What do you want, John?"

"Can I go to the bathroom?"

She sneered, then responded, really fast, "*Can* you? I don't know if you *can*. But if you want to ask to use the lavatory you ask, '*May* I,' and no, you may not."

(Excuse me, reader, but MAY I break the fourth wall here and say this crazy teacher bitch is nuts?)

Thirty seconds later, John's hand rose toward the ceiling again – this time waving frantically.

Our teacher, noticing him again – along with the rest of us in the classroom – asked, "Yes John, what is it now?"

"*May* I please use the lavatory?"

"Are you finished with drawing your five letter Os?"

"No," John replied miserably, squeezing his legs together.

And that, we all know, is the universal sign for, 'Damn I gotta goooo!'

She turned her attention to the entire class. "Listen up, all of you. No one is to use the bathroom, get a drink of water or leave this room at all until you've completely finished this assignment. Have I made myself clear?"

"Yes," we all said together.

What happens next? *I've* got to go to the bathroom. But I'm finished with my Os. That means I'll be allowed to leave. That realization gave me mixed feeling about this altogether. I *do* have to go to the lavatory, but clearly not as badly as John. I found it difficult to flaunt my permission to use the restroom in front of another suffering comrade. Now I'm getting angry at this mean teacher throwing invisible treat bombs at my gang of fools. How dare she! Not on my watch.

Rather than ask for permission to use the lavatory, I commenced to deliberately pissing all over my brown corduroy pants. I was thinking, *Come over here now, teacher, and clean my piss. As a matter of fact, clean all of our piss-stained pants. That's what you get for being so mean to us. We all pissed our pants! Hahaha!*

I had thought that, but reality showed up a second later, turning my bravery into fear.

Knowing I was the only one in the room feeling warm pee turn cold running down my leg, I began to cry.

The teacher noticed what happened and came over to me. "Why didn't you just get up and use the bathroom?"

"You said no one was allowed to use the restroom 'til we've finished," I said through my tears.

"I didn't say that."

"Yes you did," I insisted. "John had to go and you said no. Right, John?" I looked over at him for some good old-fashion support. But his retreating eye contact immediately shot me down; he went back to finishing his Os.

Thanks a lot, John!

I cried all the way to the nurse's office to await my foster mom bringing me a new pair of britches.

While we waited, the nurse asked what happened. So I told her the truth. I said we were all being held captive and weren't allowed to go to the bathroom until we finished drawing our Os.

The nurse left the room and headed straight to the principal's office. Then in came my foster mom with new duds, and I answered her questions the same as before. But I felt like she didn't believe me.

I changed in the bathroom. When I came out, the principal came in and asked if we would join him in his office. We followed him into his office and were greeted by the nurse and a surprise guest. Yup, the teacher.

"Now, Darren," the principal asked. "Would you please tell us what happened in class earlier?"

Yessss!! I screamed in my thoughts. *You're going down girl. You can't be treating little kids that way. You're bad and I'm gonna expose you!* So I told my side of the story a third time, not changing a single word.

When I finished, the principal asked the teacher if this was true.

"No. Not at all," she said, trying to sound like all goodness and light. "My students know they may use the lavatory any time. Especially in an emergency."

Oh! No! She didn't! I thought.

Now my foster mother is looking embarrassed; the principal's got this *What's wrong with you, kid?* look on his face. The teacher isn't even looking at me. But the nurse, she's got the best poker face of all.

The principal apologized to everyone but me, and excused us all. My foster mother left, but before I went back to class, the nurse called me into her office and closed the door behind us.

She knelt down in front of me, tucked in my shirt, then leaned toward me and whispered, "If you ever need my help, you come to me."

I hugged her so hard I practically choked myself.

Later that same night, around 3 a.m., I awoke to piss-soaked pajama pants. From then on, I was a bona fide bed wetter 'til the age of 13.

Visitation with Mummy

Back in the 1970s, the U.S. government was changing drastically (in a positive way) in its policies regarding the treatment of orphans and foster children. For me, and for every orphan kid after me, this was awesome.

Mummy wasn't able to care for us, but to the best of my knowledge, if she worked with her counselor and tried to stop being sick, my brothers and sister and I would be able to go back home. The welfare system set up a visitation program for us all, once every two months, to visit with each other on the North Side of Pittsburgh.

My caseworker would usually pick me up from school at 9:45 a.m. on visitation day, to get me downtown by 11 o'clock to visit with Mummy, Billy, Ricky and Lisa.

Because the rest of us kids were scattered all over Pittsburgh in different foster homes, and Billy was with the Numers, it took awhile for some of us to arrive – and sometimes only half the family would show up. But not me. I made every visit, come hell or high water.

On visitation day, the day would usually start off with me sitting in school in my morning class, surrounded by eager students ready to learn something new. Not me. I was in a relationship with the clock on the wall to my left, awaiting that 9:45 a.m. I would truly try to avoid looking at the clock 'til around 9:30 a.m. After that, the countdown was on.

My teacher's voice turned into Charlie Brown's teacher. I couldn't understand a word she said and, frankly,

16

I didn't want to. It was nothing personal; I believed I was never coming back to these strangers after every family visit. I would think that every single time. Hell, I didn't stop thinking that until I was in my 20s, as if a light bulb just turned on in my head about my Mummy's sickness and how we would never get back together under one roof again.

But back to that clock. It would be 9:44 a.m. and my enthusiasm must have shown every time. I know my heart was pounding like mad. Then the clock would turn to 9:45 and I would wait for the principal to knock on our classroom door to announce the departure of the 9:45 Darren Timothy Numer flight out of here.

Then the clock would turn to 9:46 a.m., and the beginning stages of panic would set in. Doubt began to take front row, then fear, then, *Oh God*, I'd say to myself, *Darren, don't you start crying in front of these kids, they're trying to get an education. Don't, don't, don't you dare cry,* as my eyes began to fill up without permission. Then the *knock* came! Whew, that was close.

The principal opened the door and looked straight at me. "Darren, it's time to go; your caseworker is here."

The teacher excused me, and off I went – like a bullet. Goodbye, smelly school hallway, goodbye, water fountain that always squirted me in my face, goodbye grey-and-white checkered-linoleum floor. Goodbye, super-duper heavy double-door entrance way. I'm outta here!

My caseworker put me up front in the car, next to her, seat belts buckled and all.

After an hour ride in her orange Volkswagen, we'd arrive. I would walk up five stairs, open the door and in the lobby sitting area – most of the time – was Mummy. Sitting in a chair with her head down, hands folded, legs crossed at the ankles, not reaching the floor, just waiting. A short but kind of big girl, with long dark brown hair all the way down her back. Her appearance changed in the few years we were apart, but not those blue eyes; and her beautiful smile showed up each time she saw me.

She'd say, "There's my baby. Come here and give Mummy a kiss."

I was already under her arms, holding on for dear life, looking up into her eyes awaiting my kiss on the lips.

Our visitation would take place in an area upstairs for an hour. But we each would try to stay in the lobby 'til we were all together, then we would march upstairs as a family. Lisa would show up, Ricky would show up, Billy would show up and Grandma Dobis, Mummy's mum. She was a lovely woman with moxie. She and Mummy would take turns letting me sit on their laps. Grandma usually brought a cake or donuts. It seemed like we were always celebrating one of our birthdays. The room we were in was shaped like a letter U. We were surrounded by dark-brown wood paneling, and in the room was a small round table with short chairs around it. Around the other side of the room were toys and children's books. When the grownups were talking, Lisa and I were always asked to go and play on the other side. During these visits, we mostly talked about our heritage. Mummy and Billy loved bringing up the fact on one side of our family was an angry German grandfather, and on another side we were related to the Lakota Sioux Indians through our great-grandfather. This little fact later proved beneficial to my sister in getting a job with the U.S. Postal Service when she was raising her three boys.

It seemed as soon as the visitation began, it was over. These visits always ended with me asking Mummy, "Are you still sick? You don't look sick. What can I do to make you feel better? Am I making you sick?"

She would say, "It's not that kind of sick, honey, but maybe in a few months I'll be better."

Many times during visitation, Ricky would pull me aside and try to tell me, "Look, Darren, Mummy's crazy. She'll never be well. Don't you get it?"

No I didn't. I never did, not for a long time.

So we would dry our eyes, go our separate ways. And I would try to hold my breath for two months, 'til we were all back together again, as a family.

Hangin' with the Neighborhood Kids on Dallett Road

Time to meet the neighborhood gang! For the next seven years Dallett Road in Whitehall Township would be my new home. This picturesque, middle-class Norman-Rockwell neighborhood would lend itself as learning blocks for me. I lived on a street block that housed 10 kids at least, ages ranging from three to 16. All white kids. I wasn't used to that. I won't use their last names out of privacy; plus, we've never contacted each other as adults, not that I haven't tried.

My introduction to the neighborhood kids took place in the middle of the street one hour before dinner, playing kickball with the gang. My foster dad had to pry me from the house at first. Then he took me to where everyone was, and they greeted me cheerfully and we were immediately friends.

The three sisters – Carol, Janet, and Diane, the youngest – said to me, "Come on, Darren, you're on our team," and the fun began.

Many games – like stickball, softball, football and Frisbee – were held in our private Dallett Road arena. But kickball was my favorite. I was one of the smallest kids on our block and I'd be reminded of this by Ricky, my very own bully; but I, would transform into the biggest hero when someone would accidentally kick the ball under a car. Because of my incredibly tiny stature, it was I, and only I, who dared to crawl under the greasy cars to retrieve the sport apparatus. "Ah, thank you, thank you. I'll take my bow, now."

My house was almost in the middle of the block. Across the street lived little Kelly. Down the street were the sisters (Carol, Janet and Diane). Across the street from them were Roy and his way-younger sister. Next door to them were Lori and Jon. Then three houses down were Shannon and little Ryan.

Last, waaay up the street, was my bully Ricky. He and Little Kelly's dad used to pick on me when no one was looking. I don't know when the insults started, but the colorful nicknames the two of them bestowed upon me appeared pretty much right away: "Hey Dumb-Dumb. Come here, Stupid," and this good old one, "What are you doing, Dummy?"

But the very first one putdown nickname was in Greek or Latin form, "Be-he." I think it's supposed to mean baby, and it came from Ricky's older brother, whose name I couldn't care less about remembering.

Ricky was only older than me by less than a year, you'd think he'd want to play nice. Nope. And I didn't like it one bit, either. However I did enjoy taking the upper hand, knowing that when other neighbors were around (especially my foster parents), my bullies would treat me extra kind.

I don't know how this could possibly be, but I always felt a little sorry for my bullies in life. Something must have been bothering them so badly that they had to take it out on me. I knew about this behavior because I displayed it once, myself. But I'd try never again to behave that way after the mental hurt I put on a little girl one time.

Next to the three sisters down the street were two younger kids, a boy and his younger sister, who moved away shortly after I moved on to Dallett Road. I don't remember their names, but the little girl I remember was the toast of the town. Everybody loved that little darling. Everyone but me, that is. That alone conjured a jealousy in my head. So one evening, just after the sun went down, I was alone with this little girl, and I wanted to scare her away so I could be everyone's best friend. Mind you I was a big kid of 6 and I think she was 4.

I said something like, "You know, the other kids don't like you; they're just pretending to like you."

She started crying. Man, that little kid had a set of lungs on her!

At that moment I was scared and disappointed with myself – and yes, hoping like hell she wouldn't tell her mom.

I calmed her down and begged her to not tell anyone. I said, "I was just kidding, ha ha ha!"

I don't think she ever did tell on me, because her mom was really nice to me; they even had me over to color Easter eggs once. That little girl really was the toast of the town. But, damn my behavior! I don't think I ever treated a human like that ever again; but I'd witness it myself many more times.

In the neighborhood, I was closest with the girls, mostly with Janet and Diane, Lori and her kid brother Jon. Diane and I were the same age; Lori and Janet were two years older. We were definitely Musketeers. When we weren't playing or riding our bikes in the street, we were on each other's porches, playing board games or card games: Monopoly; Sorry; Hungry-Hungry Hippos; War. You name it and among all of us, we had it all.

Now this was Pittsburgh; we had hills. So when the wintertime came, we had a blast sledding down our sloping backyards. Lori and Jon's yard had the best hills, by far. They had a double-dip hill. Yahoooooo! Such fun.

Then, when spring came, we would play in Lori and Jon's sandbox in the backyard, or play my favorite game, make believe. This game was fueled by TV shows we had previously watched. We would re-enact episodes of *Bewitched*, *Happy Days*, *Sonny and Cher*...

Ricky the bully never liked to play make believe. If the game didn't have a ball in it, he wasn't having any of it.

But I was. I *loved* it!

Oh my, I forgot about another kid on our block; his name was Stevie. He was a smaller and younger kid than me but an outgoing young sprout. His mother used to be a New York Rockette, which was probably why she used to put Stevie in plays and shows. Secretly, I was jealous. Now that I think about it, his mother was short, so maybe she wasn't with the Rockettes. She always wore high heels, which raised eyebrows among the neighbors. I do remember in their home were pictures of her in dance outfits, posing. She was awfully pretty.

One summer, Stevie was in a production of *Annie*, outdoors at a park. I remember wanting to be on that stage myself so badly, I found it hard to even sit in the audience.

You may be asking why I didn't say something to my foster mother about wanting to act. Well, I knew I couldn't ask my foster mother for anything because, after a few days of living with her, it dawned on me: I wasn't her type of kid. She would have preferred a kid like Ricky, my bully. Ricky was a tough kid, a straight-A student who loved sports. The polar opposite of me. I don't know if there was a particular moment when this realization took place. Maybe it was in our very first handshake. It was in her eyes. I recognized the hurt and pain in them when we first met, caused by what? I'll never know. Sure, she smiled; but the impression that came to me was, "Look kid, I don't know how long I'm gonna have to put up with you, but let's try to make the best of this."

Decades later I learned the Hearts were unable to have children of their own; so I'm pretty sure that had to have played a part in it.

Mrs. Heart stayed to herself a lot. I was almost never allowed to have friends in the house. If there was a block party, neither of my foster parents would come and join in the festivities. I didn't get it. God, every day I tried to produce a party.

She'd always say to me, "Go out and play, go out

and play," and God forbid if it was raining! Then she was forced to share her house with me.

Now, please understand, I've got good things to say about this lady. My absolute favorite memory with her were the times when we watched *Little House On The Prairie* together. Yes it'd be raining outside, and boy, were those episodes tearjerkers! At the end of the show, we would cry in front of the TV together. Then we looked at each other and started to laugh. It was a bonding moment I'll always cherish.

Accidental Thief

After a few years in the summertime, for the gang and me, a store run up to the Whitehall Shopping Center would be our biggest adventure. Back then in that shopping center there was a milk store, Baskin-Robbins Ice Cream, Mellon Bank, a Sears for the rich people and a Woolworth's for the blue-collar workers. It was a treat to go into Sears. You got dressed up back then to go in there. Oh, and a movie theatre, too. A McDonald's would show up a few years later.

We'd make the quarter-mile hike up and down those hills in order to refill our gallon jugs of milk for our individual families. The march to the store was musical and magical, musical because we would bang the empty gallon drums on our knees and it made the best bong sound. The magic was from our friendship. At the milk store we would get our new milk while trading in our old empty milk-drum containers. The full milks were heavy. Man, were they heavy!

One particular time, I didn't have to get milk, but the girls did. Before we left to return home, we stopped by Woolworth's to see what the latest hit record was. We would also play one round of Space Invaders and get a piece of candy with our leftover change. I picked up the latest 45 record; it was "Eye of The Tiger," by Survivor.

I went over to find the girls at the candy section. We were having too much fun. They paid for their candy and we left. Around four blocks away I realized I hadn't paid for this record I clearly had accidentally stolen. We all stared at each other for what seemed an eternity.

I broke the silence, shrugged my shoulders and said, "Eh, they're not gonna miss it."

I offered to carry their milk home, and did so; but they refused to touch the stolen merchandise. That was the quietest walk home ever!

To this day every time I hear that song, back down memory lane I go. I don't know why I didn't take it back. But the thrill became a game for me, and this disease would not leave my body 'til my late 20s after two trips to the slammer. One thing I learned: You want to know who's a true friend? Ask them to come and visit you in jail.

Summer Fun at the Pool

Alright, we're strolling down memory lane in summertime, right? What goes better in the summer than a hot-dog stand next to a ballpark? A hot-dog stand next to the community pool. *Oh, yeah!* Our community Whitehall Swimming Pool is where I ruled. Actually, the hot-dog stand wasn't next to the pool; it was around back, down under the pool, kind of. And it wasn't just hot dogs, either; we're talking about frozen orange push-ups, soda pop, vanilla or chocolate ice-cream bars, and *candy*! My favorite were the Swedish Fish.

But back to my swimming pool, throughout the years here, I would learn a lot: how to run on cement in flip flops – because without them you were sure to stub and gash your big toe. Cut it open and begin bleeding. Then you would have to walk all the way to the nurses' aid station on your heel. After they bandaged you up, you couldn't go back in the pool for the rest of the day. Huge bummer.

At my pool, I would also learn patience. I'd learn how to stand in line for the low dive. Within a few more years, I'd learn how to do a double flip. I was a flippin' fool, in more ways than one. I learned how to smoke there, too – and saw my first pair of boobs.

Her name was Michelle. I pulled her bathing suit top down once... well, maybe twice. The cigarette-smoking lessons came from Michelle's friends, who were seniors. They were the cool kids, and I wanted in.

27

Years later I would run into Michelle at a college party. But let's not get ahead of ourselves.

Toward the end of my stay with the Hearts, I would discover my sexuality. I was smitten by Scott, the college-age lifeguard at my pool. He could have been the twin to the actor in the movie *Blue Lagoon*, Christopher Atkins, starring opposite Brooke Shields.

He would blow spit bubbles off his tongue from his lifeguard chair. We kids were fascinated with that. Somehow, he could form a bubble of spit on the edge of his tongue and blow it off. And, he showered naked. Thank you, Scott, for that one. I didn't shower naked with him too often. I couldn't for technical puberty reasons. I'm sure he knew I had a crush on him. But hell, we all did!

My first day at the pool, from my first swimming lesson, I was hooked.

You know how I used to love hiding? Well, I had discovered a new place to hide: under water. It would only be weeks 'til I could swim all the way to the deep end – 12 feet deep. I went through two sets of tubes in my ears because I would never put in my ear plugs.

Did I mention I had a love affair with the diving board? The low dive, we were best friends. The high dive? She was extra, extra wasabi on your sushi! I loved her. As an adult, I've gone back to visit that Whitehall swimming pool and she's still beautiful as can be, with her gorgeous blue waters. The low dive is still there; however, the high dive has been retired and has been turned into a medium dive. Sorry about that, old girl. You sure did lift me up and sometimes you kicked my ass; but I promise, you are missed.

Six Months in a Cast... and Not the Theatrical Kind

Around the time I was in third grade, my bedwetting problem landed me in the hospital. It was really getting on my foster parents' nerves. Can you blame them, though? Pissy, smelly sheets *every night*... and that damn plastic bottom bed sheet that crinkled all night long.

Around that same time I realized I was being taken to an awful lot of psychologists. I think they thought my bed wetting was a mental thing. At least, I hope that's what they were thinking, and not "The kid's crazy, right, Doc?" Ahh, who am I kidding? It's all of the above.

When all the various therapists' ink blots couldn't stop my floods at night, off to the hospital we went.

As soon as the doctors returned from behind the giant x-ray machine, the "crazy" verdict on my disobedient potty-patrol midnight parties went right out the window.

And that's when they discovered I had scoliosis – a deformed curvature of the spine. An operation was added to our agenda immediately. Two surgical choices loomed. The first was to place a steel bar in my back, which would be there forever. The second choice (the one my foster parents decided on) was a new concept. The surgeons would take slivers of bone from each of my shins. Those slivers would be inserted into my back. I would have to wear a full body cast for six months. After that, I had to wear a back brace for a bunch of years later. It was the same kind of brace the Hollywood actress Lisa Kudrow wore in the movie, *Romy and Michele's High School Reunion*.

I got permission from my doctor, then asked my foster dad to cut the plastic chin piece off. I covered the visible metal neck brace thingy with a bandana. Then, as far as I knew, my back brace was completely hidden. My bandana collection still thrives today – just like my brother Billy's.

It was my foster mom's decision to not have a steel bar permanently placed in my back. I may have heard her say, "The boy's addicted to cartwheels, Doctor; he won't be able to fly with a steel rod holding him down."

Thank you for that, Mrs. Heart!

I lived in the hospital for what seemed like forever: lying in bed in a full-body cast that stretched from my neck all the way to my knees. At the end of my stay was when I got into my first and only fight with my foster dad.

He was teaching me how to play Tic-Tac-Toe, and I was 0-for 10. I mean, I was losing big time. I was getting mad that I knew – and he knew – I wasn't going to win.

Mr. Heart noticed I was starting to cry. "Why are you crying?" he asked.

I banged my fist on my tray table. "You never let me win!"

He started laughing. "That's the point. You have to want to win. I can't just let you win. I'm not gonna do that, nosiree, Bob. If I let you win, you'll become accustomed to it, and that won't help you one bit when you're older, no sir," he said. "Plus, look on the bright side, kid" – he never called me son, he'd only called me his foster son when introducing me to anyone, they both did – "you're coming home tomorrow, and the ambulance is taking you home tomorrow morning, they're going to put on the siren and lights for you."

And they did. I remember that, that cool gray rainy morning on my face. They wheeled my hospital bed into the living room, where I'd stay for about six months.
After my foster dad said all that, we played three more games of Tic-Tac-Toe. I'd like to say I won at least one of

them. But I can't. I lost all three games. I turned my head away and shed one more silent tear before falling asleep. I'm much older now since that game of Tic-Tac-Toe. Mr. Heart, thank you. I'm winning now.

Kisses, a Flip Over and an Attempted Visit

So now I'm bedridden *and* a bed wetter. Gee, lucky me... and lucky Mr. and Mrs. Heart. I hope they put a diaper on me. If they did, trust me, I've completely blocked it all out. What 8- or 9-year-old kid wants that as a memory? Lying on my back in the living room was fun for one day only. Three memory moments stuck with me in those months: kisses, a flip over and my brother Ricky.

The kisses came from a request I'd made. I became really sad after watching my foster parents kissing only each other night after night before heading to bed, and I wanted in on the action. Again I would be crying softly in my open-casket hospital bed with my head turned away.

"What's the matter?" Mrs. Heart asked.

In the lightest whisper ever, I asked, "Why don't you two ever kiss me good night?"

"What?" she asked. "I can't hear you."

So I upped the volume – and that irritated me by itself, because now I know I'm begging for a falsehood. Still not looking at her I asked, "Why don't I get any kisses before bedtime?"

Mrs. Heart didn't say a word. She stared at me for a second, then she leaned over my bed rail and kissed my forehead. It sucked, but if I was forced to play this type of Tic-Tac-Toe this way, I'm in it to win. She went to bed and about a minute later Mr. Heart came to the side of my adult-size crib and kissed me on the head and said good-night, then went upstairs to bed.

I didn't cry myself to sleep anymore after that. It

was time to grow up, even while I was stuck lying down.

The flip-over memory came toward the end of my body-cast adventure. I was bored as hell, as always. I mean no disrespect to the many, many hours of *Sesame Street*, *Mr. Rogers' Neighborhood* and the *Electric Company*. Thank you, PBS, really. Thank you. But on this particular day I was fidgety and wanted to get up and get out. My Lego blocks were right below me, under the hospital bed. I was able to lean on my side and could look down and see them. Sooo, if I was able to get onto my side, I thought, *Well, maybe I could just get on my knees and lean forward over the bed rail and reach down and get my Legos.*

There I was, on my knees, starting to lean forward. Then I was teetering for a second. Before I knew it, I had flipped over the railing and made a loud crash onto the floor. Mrs. Heart came running from the kitchen. Without a word, she bent down and scooped me off the floor and placed me back in bed.

When I was settled back in the bed, she asked, "Are you alright?"

"Yeah," I replied. Now, where she got the strength to pick me up, I don't know.

This last memory comes from my brother, Ricky. I vaguely remember it. He said one time when he had run away from a foster home (which he did many times), he had heard I was in a body cast so he decided to come all the way over and visit me. But when he got there, Mrs. Heart didn't even let him in the front door. Ricky told me this story when I was in my late 20s. For some reason, I kind of remember him leaning to the side to look around and past Mrs. Heart, and our eyes locked. But that's all I got before he was told to leave.

Looking back, I remember the neighbor kids would come over and visit and show me how they learned cursive writing skills. That infuriated me because, lucky me, I was still working on that damn letter O! I did have a tutor sent from school from time to time. However, my education was falling backward about as fast as I'd fallen out of bed. But I didn't care; this body cast was coming off soon, and I was gonna be on my feet running... or so I thought.

The big day arrived. At the hospital, they'd taken that itchy old full-body cast off, but the nurses wouldn't let me walk.

"We have to get an x-ray first," they told me as they sat me in a wheelchair.

Back to that loud, buzzing room we went.

In the light-green room, they carefully stood me up and asked me if I could hold onto the two bars against the x-ray wall, so they could get an image of my back.

"Sure," I said. "No problem."

But when they let go of me, I couldn't support my body. My legs had shut down completely.

Fortunately, the nurses caught me before I hit the floor.

They straightened my legs and instructed me to stand up, if I could.

I could not. Floppy wet noodles had replaced my legs!

I went to my fallback position: I started to cry.

The nurses calmed me down, reassuring me this was natural. They explained it happened because I'd been off my feet for so long. It was something called "muscle atrophy."

My strength eventually showed up. They got their x-ray taken, then we went straight to physical therapy.

Within a few weeks' time, I was running all over the place – an 8-year-old superhero with a brand-new back brace. At least that's how I felt. It sounds strange, but I didn't view my back brace as a drawback or even a dunce cap; rather, it had more of a superhero's cape feel to me.

Then again, maybe I didn't need apparatus to feel like a superhero. Even as a kid, I'd take it upon myself to try to right the world's wrongs... beginning with taking on bullies.

Righting Wrongs as a Second-Grade Superhero

Back in my second-grade class. I was sitting close to the back of the room and, unbeknownst to the rest of the class, the two boys in front of me were fighting over an eraser. The kid directly in front of me was in the wrong; he wouldn't return the eraser he'd borrowed from the other boy. Their quarrel grew so intense, I was starting to shake. Suddenly a fight erupted. They were on the floor, punching and hitting each other over this little bitty eraser.

And I was going to save that other kid's pride, and rescue his eraser from the bully. I clenched both my fists and held my right hand up high to the Gods. I leapt out of my chair – like a frog's tongue to a midnight dragonfly. I pounced on the offender and bopped him on his head, then jumped back into my seat. (Hey, I didn't want to get caught fighting.)

All of a sudden the bully started crying, and I was thinking, *Yeah, mess with bull, you'll get the horns.* Oh, how prophetic that thought would be! For there stood, in front of us all, a crying little boy… with an upside-down #2 pencil sticking straight up from the top of his head. Damn, I'd forgotten to put my pencil down! As for my punishment, I had to stay in for recess that day. The injured kid was sent to the nurse's office for a much-needed Band-Aid. And the other kid? He never did send me a thank-you card.

The Word of the Day

The day I got caught playing doctor with little Kelly across the street, things got blown way out of proportion. But let me back up a month or so, to fill in the blanks. I was like 11 or 12 years old and the sisters, Janet and Diane, were babysitting little Kelly across the street. They invited me into the house and took me straight up to Kelly's room, leaving the kid downstairs by herself.

Diane sat with me on the bed. She looked over at Janet and said, "Go get it."

Janet left the room and returned with what looked like a six-inch square flat box, with pretty colors on it.

"So what? Big deal," I said.

Diane clamped a hand over my mouth "Shh!" she hissed.

"No, look at the cover of the box," Janet urged in a whisper.

The best way I can describe what I first saw would be what looked like a Gianni Versace printed scarf (although Versace wouldn't be heard of for another 10 more years). All I could make out was busy colors – light orange and yellow abstract shapes – and swirling paisleys.

"Don't you *see* it?" they asked together.

"No, I still don't see it. And frankly, I couldn't care less. This game sucks!"

And their next question changed the playing field forever in my life.

"Can't you see all the people?" Diane was grinning.

I looked closer. Then I saw it. There was one face, then another, and another and another, and another. They looked happy. I noticed they seemed to be lying awfully close together, but they sur did look happy. Then – oh my God! – I realized something. *They're not wearing any clothes!* He's on top of her, she's on top of him. What is that thing in her mouth?! Oh my God, it's *him* in her mouth.

Wow! Now what's this thing growing down in my pants?

In a panic I stared at the two of them. "I gotta go!" I exclaimed, jumping up off the bed.

I ran down the stairs, out of the house, across the street and went straight to bed, my head spinning. That was my first introduction to the birds and the bees. What an intro, on an 8-mm XXX film box! That picture still won't leave my head to this day. The word of the day, boys and girls, is "orgy."

Playing Doctor

Now back to when I got busted playing doctor with little Kelly in her folks' basement. They had the best basement playroom – it was carpeted and everything! Her dad may have been a prick, but he was really handy with a hammer.

Now that I knew what naked people looked like, I had to know what Kelly's hot dad looked like – specifically, what his ding-a-ling looked like. So we started to play the strip-off-your-clothes-in-the-small-closet-and-ask-each-other-private-questions game. Her questions were all about me, but my questions were all about her dad.

She mentioned when she was younger they used to take showers together. So naturally I asked what color his ding dong was.

She said, "Purple."

That must have been the safe word, because at that moment I heard the basement door open and Kelly's mom was coming down the stairs in a big hurry. Thank God we got our pants up, but we didn't get our shirts on fast enough.

That was it. I was immediately kicked out of all the reindeer games on that block, for a long time. But my time was running short with the Hearts anyhow. I guess things were working out for everyone in the long run.

The Hearts weren't big on kisses and hugs. But whenever I got physically hurt, that's when the Love would show. I remember they had these life-size cement deer in the backyard and I was by myself, rocking the tall standing one back and forth, until it fell over on me and pinned my leg against the tree.

I screamed, "Mom!"

Mrs. Heart rescued me. She lifted up the deer, picked me up and carried me to the car and drove me to the hospital. I felt such warmth in those moments. I Loved being carried in her arms. In the seven years I spent with Mr. and Mrs. Heart, I fractured both my legs, cracked my wrist while skateboarding and managed to bang my head against something at least once a year. What we do for Love, huh?

Throwing Away My Future... From the School Bus Window

The breaking point with the Hearts came on the school bus (which was my favorite part of the school day, actually, because I had my own personal captive audience). But I'd like to share one other story before I get to that.

This one time on our school bus, a classmate was being picked on because she and her big sister were new to the school. The younger girl was my age; her name was Wendy. I can't remember the other sister's name but she was a beautiful teen model from New York and they were Jewish. I hadn't a clue what Jewish was, but just the day before we were all getting along beautifully on the bus – even singing!

I loved getting the whole bus to sing, all the time. "O How Happy You Have Made Me," or "Lean on Me," we'd sing. But not today. A big bully girl tried to pick on these two Jewish girls, but I wasn't having it – not on *my* bus.

I stood up and shouted, "So what? So what if they're different? They're our new friends and friends don't do that to friends." I remember complimenting the bully on how smart she was and how dumb it is, not being nice to someone.

To my surprise, it worked, because she made friends with them.

However, a winter season later, I would accidentally throw a snowball high in the air, aiming to hit one of the sisters way across the street, just for fun. Well I did that, alright. I hit Wendy's older sister – right in the eye. Now, remember, she was a model. They and their folks were at my house so fast to tell on me, there was nowhere for me to hide! It was an accident – but try telling that to people who are getting tired of you. It's impossible.

The straw that broke the camel's back came a few weeks later.

On the school bus, we kids had developed a bad habit of throwing spitballs out the window. But spitballs eventually became little rocks, which turned into bigger rocks. Not to be outdone on my bus, one day I threw out a combination lock. It happened to hit the windshield of an oncoming car. And it was just my luck we had a police car behind us! Yes, we got pulled over. No, none of us said a word when asked who threw the lock out the window.

As it turned out, the daughter of the guy whose car I hit was on our bus. Small world, huh?

The following morning, in homeroom, I wrote a full-page apology letter to the principal, unsigned. In it I stated I would somehow pay for the damage, but begged him not to say anything to my foster folks. I had a friend deliver my letter to the office, asking him to just drop it off and not say it was from me.

Less than two minutes later, over the loudspeaker system of Painter Middle school, I heard my name being called out… to report to the principal's office.

When I got there, the principal was ready to paddle me again, but I stopped him.

"I'm a foster child. You're not allowed to hit me anymore."

I'd learned that little tidbit a few weeks earlier, from my caseworker. I had told her Mr. Heart had paddled me for leaving our street block without permission and coming home that night late. The caseworker told me, "Darren, no one is to ever lay a hand on you, *ever*."

When I got home from school that day, Mrs. Heart came up to me and got right up in my face, quoting the exact words I spewed to the principal earlier – only with a *lot* more sarcasm.

"You can't paddle me 'cause I'm a foster kid," she mocked. I can still remember the sneer on her face. "Go to your room! Don't come down 'til we call for you."

The next morning, the sun wasn't even up yet, but Mr. Heart woke me up. He said, "Darren, get dressed and come downstairs."

As I got dressed, I could slightly hear the sound of another person in the house.

As I neared the bottom of the stairs, I saw my caseworker standing in the front doorway. She looked up at me with a sad expression on her face. I glanced to my right and saw a large black trash bag on top of the dining-room table.

Odd, I thought, *why would there be a full bag of grass cuttings on the dining-room table? Oh, wait, I know what that is…*

Mr. Heart picked up the bag, handed it to my caseworker and opened the door for us – and my belongings – to exit.

I didn't look at the Hearts and I didn't say a word. I finished those last three steps down the stairs. It began to rain. Really? How fucking ironic. I cried so hard the entire two-hour drive back to the McIntyre Shelter! Harder even than the rain that pelted the windshield the whole way. I even cried in the Denny's restaurant, into my lunch that I had no appetite for.

But I did smoke the cigarettes I asked my caseworker to buy for me.

Later that day, I was delivered to Cottage 5.

That night, I called the Hearts to see if I could come back to their home.

Mr. Heart said, "No."

I hung up and Miss Linda, our cottage monitor, a big Italian woman, held me tight and let me cry again.

Smells in My Dreams

Did you ever smell smells in your dreams? I did as a child, back when I was living with the Hearts. I would often wake up remembering and asking myself, *Where is that smell from?* Was it something someone was cooking? No. I never knew, but that smell was in my dreams.

The answer came that first night I went back to the McIntyre Shelter. After I cried under Miss Linda's arms, she gave me two more hugs all by herself, while hiding her tears.

She said to me, "It's time to go to bed honey, it's getting late."

She led me to the corridor that leads to the upstairs where all us orphan kids would sleep. As I climbed the stairs, a familiar, odorous old friend came back to visit my long-awaiting nostrils. It was the smell of the second-floor cottages. I was dream smelling, they smelled like this, of course, the showers, the dirty clothes, the clean clothes and the smell of the individual kids all swarming together.

Hey old friend, you've been in my dreams for years. How the hell have you been? You still stink a little, but boy, have I missed you. Without knowing it, I was home again.

That following morning came quickly, as I moved slowly. I looked all around the room I had just slept in. I looked at the two-light green woolly blanketed springy steel beds, the two dark brown divider cabinets that separated our beds from the other side of the room and its two beds. I looked out my four huge windows, down the steep

43

hill and across the highway; there was a shopping center.

A few kids were still upstairs with me; they poked their heads in my room but didn't say hi. They just ran off, yelling, "Breakfast is ready!"

As I made my way downstairs toward the dining room, the noise of the boys was growing louder. I turned the corner into the room; there they all were, my new brothers, mostly black kids, devouring breakfast cereal as fast as they could. I soon learned, the first one done eating got to choose the cartoon to watch in the TV room before school. *Casper the Friendly Ghost* usually won. If you weren't in the mood for TV, there was always the pool room. With chalk, sticks, balls and all… although, a lot of times some kid would hide the eight ball just to be mean.

When you've been raised like a tennis ball – knocked from one side of the court to the other – you learn really fast who's got game and who doesn't. I was about to meet my match that morning.

My First Real Best Friend

After breakfast, I noticed this kid, this dark colored-skin kid. Aside from his color, Lamar was just like me. Same age, same height, smart, witty, popular – and he had that look in his eye. And I knew we were gonna fist fight soon. I don't know why. I said something he said something and before you knew it, we were fighting.

I swear, a few times in my life, this slow-motion feeling took over my world. This was one of those times. He was swinging his arms, I was swinging my arms. I was amazed neither of us was wanting to hurt the other. I even think I heard him giggle a little, too. We both knew the counselor on duty was going to break us up, so why end the fight? Let's give our fellow brothers a show right here in the hallway.

After that morning's fake fight, the two of us were inseparable. Lamar was my first real best friend.

He turned me on to Marlboro cigarettes.

"Everyone here smokes Newports, so if you smoke what they don't like, they won't bum your smokes from you," he told me.

Plus they weren't called cigarettes; they called them squares.

I'll admit for the last seven years I was living in a *Leave it to Beaver* white-bread neighborhood. But being back here at the shelter, I heard stories from other counselors.

They would come up to me, saying, "Oh, you're a Numer. We know your older brother, Ricky Numer, he's such a good kid."

That would make Ricky laugh every time; he swore he was the opposite. Whether he was good or bad, I didn't care, I was in a familiar place. Thank you, Jesus!

New Kid in McIntyre School

As much as I'd hated it during my first stay there, this time around I quickly learned McIntyre was the bomb! They had just built a brand-new school, two stories high, in front of the entranceway to the property. A big almost-square red-brick building, the new school featured large, white aluminum-trimmed, single-pane windows. The school was situated on a downhill slope, so the second floor was essentially at ground level; a walking bridge took you from the street parallel to the first floor. After crossing the bridge, you arrived at the full-glass double entry doors. Through those doors was the new nurses' offices, and half school.

In this school, the teachers must have known ahead of time they were about to be handed a big dummy of a student. They sat me down in class for the first time with everyone in there, maybe five kids to a classroom. They started teaching with a third-grade curriculum. I was in Heaven!! I was like, *Give me a test now! You best believe I can pass it....*

While I'm envisioning myself in one corner of the ring, hands clasped, raised to the stars, like a prized champ, on the other side is a defeated brother, beat down, and I never even touched him. Someone else did, though – and fucking *hard*, too! I could see the bruises all over his Soul. This must be where I learned to Love the stranger. I was 13 years old at this point. I had no clue that over the next three years I would live in two group homes and two more

47

foster families, plus get my first taste of living on the streets of Pittsburgh during a runaway extravaganza.

Now back to that classmate in the ring who isn't as smart as me. If you just snickered at that last sentence, I Love you. I feel you. We've all laughed at the dummy sometimes. At some point though, we must rise above. No, we have to bring ourselves down to give a hand up to those who will never be smarter than us. I believe this is what our teachers taught us at that school.

At that school I had two crushes. The first was Mrs. Williams, one of my teachers. She was so nice and so compassionate, I immediately felt drawn to her. I became emotionally attached to her within about three weeks of being there. I asked Mrs. Williams if she would take me home and be my foster mom. She looked like the actress Lynda Carter, from *Wonder Woman*. And she behaved like Wonder Woman, too, so can you blame me?

I've been told you don't get what you don't ask for. Plus, what's the worst that could happen? She'd say, "No," right? So I asked.

She said no, and I lost it – hard – but quietly, in my cubicle.

Ms DiLeo – and My Brush with Fame

My other school-teacher crush was Ms DiLeo.

She was medium tall and on the skinny side; she looked older but comfortable, with the kindest heart and soul, ever. She came back from a trip to California once with a stack of 8x12 copies of this one picture. It was of herself, her brother – maybe cousin, I'm not sure – Frank Michael DiLeo, and his client, Michael Jackson, whom he managed in the 1980s.

I could have died! Even at 13, I wanted so badly to be on stage, but would never have had the confidence to speak those words out loud. Then to receive that photo from a teacher I'd Loved from the word hello – who, as it turned out, was only one degree of separation from the most talented stage performer on the planet. OMG! It was like I'd died and gone to Hollywood Heaven!

I don't have that picture of her anymore, but I see it in my mind every time I think of her. Ms DiLeo was my biggest fan, and I was her "teacher's pet." I made damn sure of that.

Whenever I left McIntyre Shelter to live somewhere else for a little bit, her goodbyes were the hardest. Then I would inevitably return, and we'd round the corner to see each other all over again. She would give me this heartfelt grin that would say, *What are you doing back here?*

My eyes would say back to her, while mirroring her grin, *Shut up; you know I only came back here for you.* We were down like that.

I would describe her as kind of a cross between Princess Diana and Judge Judy – sweet and kind, but tough when she needed to be.

Then one day she pulled all of us classmates all together, told us she'd been battling cancer and had to leave for a short visit to the hospital. The last thing she said to us was, "I'll be back."

She never came back.

I was actually clueless about the word cancer. So I can only say ignorance really is bliss.

Sometime around 2009, Randy (my life partner, whom I'll talk more about later of course) and I were at the bar on Saturday noon time, but this wasn't just any bar. We were at the Beverly Hilton poolside bar, in Beverly Hills, California. We'd been there for an hour already, feeling toasty. There's this huge, rectangular, sparkling blue swimming pool with gorgeous white-linen sheers made into cabanas on one side. On the other side are hotel room entryways. There are about 10 round tables with chairs that separate the swimming pool from the bar area.

As Randy and I toasted our bar keep for the fourth time for what a beautiful morning it was, I noticed this guy who just walked in, about 50 feet away. This is the most striking, colorful peacock of a man I had ever seen. His hooded jacket boasted every color you could think of. He was my height, my size – yes, short and fat. He might have been 60, but he didn't look it. The lady with him looked amazing, too. I think she had on a gold scarf, matching her gold outfit, and an air of sophistication straight out of New York City. And did they ever have bling! Together they looked like a Hollywood couple triumphantly entering their own successful movie premier. And where was the red carpet? All around them, according to their smiles on their faces. His thinning dark hair was pulled back in a *Miami Vice* ponytail. Her eyes were scanning the view.

They went straight to the middle table, where they

began to wave at fellow patrons. To my surprise, everyone waved back. As they began to sit, they were immediately approached by this tall, stunningly handsome black guy – like Denzel-Washington good looking. Then my peacock got up and hugged him, so they obviously knew each other. Now Randy and I figured out the mystery: The tall dude's an actor, short guy's an agent. That was sure fun to watch, though. But it was time for us to leave.

I said goodbye to our bartender, then asked for directions to the restroom.

"Make a left when you get to the curved stairs, then go right and head down to the end of the orange carpeted hallway."

On my way back from that long hallway, at the bottom of those stairs, Randy was talking to that tall actor we'd been watching minutes earlier. Randy was trying to get him to be in one of our play productions. We were always doing that; hell, we still do.

Then Randy asked the question I was dying to ask: "Who was that little guy you were talking to?"

A big smile came over his face, teeth and all. "Oh, that's Frank Michael DiLeo; he used to be Michael Jackson's manager, back in the day."

I almost passed out. I always deep down believed I was gonna meet this guy Frank one day, and today looks like that day. I had to tell him how much my teacher meant to me – and how much she spoke about and loved him. But I held my composure with everything inside of me, except for the tears that started flowing uncontrollably down my face in front of this tall, beautiful young actor.

I asked him if he would tell his friend Frank one day, "A kid from Pittsburgh made it to Hollywood because of seeds his teacher, Ms. DiLeo planted in him, and he'll forever be grateful."

Okay, I know I got a little sidetracked and roundabout there, but if you were to ask me my most-favorite part about McIntyre Shelter, I'd have to say Ms DiLeo.

Running Away

What was my second most favorite part about McIntyre Shelter? Running away!

I ran away from there so many times, I came really close to being thrown into the Shuman Juvenile Detention Center. That place was for the really bad kids! I think my brother Ricky went there once.

He used to urge me to not act up too much, "because that's a place, Darren, you don't want to go to."

But in the beginning stages of being a runaway, you go with a friend. It's like the unofficial runaway buddy system. First you go down the hill, cross the highway, try not to get hit by speeding cars. You go up to the mall, cruise the mall, steal candy and head back home before dinner, hoping you weren't seen.

But of course you were always seen. Always. Every time. Our punishment? Early to bed, and the worst part, no cigarette privileges for three days. After a few short runaway trips, it was time to see what was on the other side of the world: downtown Pittsburgh.

Our great escape began right after dinner. Down the hill and across McKnight Road. This time we followed the highway toward downtown. We walked behind the buildings, shopping centers, churches and tall billboards. It was a three or four mile hike, up and down those tall hills. And we had to hide from the cops, who'd obviously been tipped off about our escape.

We made it all the way to the North Side, with just

the Andy Warhol Bridge over the Allegheny River separating us from downtown Pittsburgh. We had to rest, though. It was close to midnight. We had snatched two cartons of smokes, a bottle of soda, a loaf of Town Talk bread (that's kind of the law in Pittsburgh, because it's our hometown bread) and a hammer for protection.

During that trip I threw that hammer up into a street light behind an abandoned building. Nailed it. We ran like hell from there after that.

So on the North Side, in the park, the six of us tried to sleep all huddled together in one of those giant, unburied cement drainage pipes, to get away from the late-night wind and cold. That didn't work out so well, so a few blocks further down the street we discovered a stairwell to a parking garage. We climbed all the way to the fifth floor, which seemed to be the warmest spot, and we slept.

After about 25 minutes, we woke up.

One of my cohorts said, "Come on, we're almost to downtown. Let's keep going."

Before we took off, some of the other kids wanted to get warm, and suggested we go to the emergency room across the park.

As soon as we entered the front door, the security guards came at us. They must have had their eyes on us all along. Four of us escaped, but the other two got caught.

From then, we laid low, not walking under street lights if we could help it, and turning our backs if we saw the law coming.

We four musketeers made it across the bridge, and before I knew it we were standing downtown with a two-story McDonald's in front of us and the giant gray KDKA TV buildings behind us. We were hungry, and we needed money.

So one of my comrades – a girl – said, "Come on, we gotta beg for money."

I'd never begged before and I had no idea how.

"Just hold your hand out, look real sad, and ask for

just change. They get pissed if ya ask for more," she told me.

This was way scarier than the high dive ever! Your first begging gig is the hardest. Truly, the strength to lift that arm up from the elbow requires every ounce of energy in your world. Then you've got to cup your hand like a spoon, moving it forward an inch, slowly, so as not to scare your target. Now it's time to talk.

The phrase, "Please, could you spare a dime?" doesn't want to come out of your mouth because of the humiliating feeling deep in your gut that goes with the territory. Then the strength of an empty stomach shows up, and you fight to get the job done.

I remember scoring big on my first begging gig. He was a handsome, preppy lawyer-looking kind of guy – maybe 25 years old. He gave me a five-dollar bill. I ate good that night, I mean early, early morning.

Right after the meal, we all kind of looked at each other and asked, "What's next?"

They each had a home or a relative with loving waiting arms they wanted to go to. I had neither, but I wasn't about to let them know that. So we hugged for a long time, then went our separate ways.

I spent the next 12 hours roaming the streets of downtown Pittsburgh, high on all the city sights and sounds and the smells of all the different corner hotdog shops and cafés.

About 4 p.m., I was getting hungry. I had three bucks left from last night's beggary, and I thought if I could take a bus back to Mr. and Mrs. Heart's place, and just show up, maybe they'd take me back. I asked a stranger at a bus stop where and which bus would take me back to Whitehall Township. Of course it had to be on the other side of downtown.

I boarded the bus, heading to an old home I once knew. It had been about six months since I'd left the Hearts and their side of town. While riding the bus, I started to see familiar landmarks from the many road trips we'd taken over the years on this familiar Highway 51. I got scared I was going to pass their house; in a panic I got off the bus at the next stop. Wrong move! I was two miles short of my destination, and the snow and rain had started up.

So along the highway I trod. The sun had almost set, and my Whitehall Township Shopping Center was just up this big hill off the highway, just down the road from a Pizza Hut.

I climbed the extremely slippery, cold, wet hill. As if this trip couldn't get any worse, I had to go number two. At first I started to giggle to myself, thinking if my friends could see me now. Halfway up a hill with no leaves on the trees to hide me, bare ass, bent over, searching through the wet brown leaves to find something to wipe up with.

I pulled my pants up, began to climb the hill again, only 60 feet to go. Then I slipped and fell, clinging to wet roots and dirt to stop from sliding down the steep hillside. That's when I lost it and began to cry.

I got mad and cried out, "God, what the hell are you doing to me? I can't take this shit anymore!"

That's when it happened.

When I was living with the Hearts, there was a Mrs. Black who lived next door. This always freaked me out; here she was, the whitest old lady with the whitest hair ever and her last name was Black, Mrs. Betty Black. Boy, was she always on fire for Jesus! She even said she could talk to him, which thrilled me to no end. I asked her many times how she could talk to him.

She said, "I just listen for his voice."

Now I know when someone's bullshitting me, but I never got that feeling from her, ever.

We kids spent many, many hours on her back porch or front porch. We would play Barrel of Monkeys or those green, yellow and red Pick-Up Sticks games. During those times, she would read the Bible or talk about Jesus. I even asked Mrs. Black one time (on another runaway trip back to that neighborhood) if she would let me live with her. She went upstairs to pray about it, then came back and said no; she put a twenty-dollar bill in my hand and I left. One of her two sons even became a preacher, I heard.

Anyhow, while back on that hill I called out for her Jesus, and He – or someone, maybe the Universe – spoke to me. I started to feel warm all over, the sound of a loud whisper began to drown out the highway traffic noise far below my cold, frozen, dirty tennis shoes.

I heard, "Let me kick your butt while you're young. I will pull you through all of this when it's over. Do you trust me?"

I answered, "Yes."

Then the voice said, "I need to put you through the wringer for a while. Can you handle it?"

I said, "Yes," and got the hell out of there, 'cause that shit was spooky!

I blocked that out of my memory quickly – and for a long time afterward.

I made it to my old stomping grounds, Dallett Road. As I marched in the dark wet night, heading toward my old house, my heart began to change. I could hear or feel my attitude toward Mr. and Mrs. Heart's home.

"Don't go to their home; you will not be welcomed there," came to me.

As I walked past their house, I did my best to not even look into their place. Instead I went to Mrs. Heart's closest friend down the street. I must have been away for so long that when she answered the door she didn't even remember me; plus, I was a bit dirty.

After remembering me, finally, she welcomed me in, then called a neighbor down the street, because she said there was nothing she could do for me.

"No problem," I said, flicking my cigarette ashes into the glass ashtray she gave me. The neighbors she called were Shannon and little Ryan's folks. They lovingly took me in and took care of me, they washed my clothes and let me shower, then they welcomed in the cops to take me to the local police station, right next to my Whitehall swimming pool, where I would sit in a jail cell for the first of many times to come.

What was my first time in jail like?

I Loved it!

First Time in Jail

The police officer put me in the back of the squad car. It was like a limousine ride. I didn't have handcuffs on; I wasn't a criminal… yet. The Whitehall police station was located slightly south of the local library. When we got to the station, they held the door open for me, like I was royalty.

In the station, though, the tides of fun started to change, quickly.

Another officer came up to me and said, "Kid we're gonna have to put you in the back. Sorry about that, but we've got nowhere else to put you."

Oh, crap! They're talking about putting me behind bars, I know it.

They walked me to the back, behind a large wooden door with a thick window with wire lace in the glass. Through that door, there they were: three empty jail cells, with gray-painted bars and gray-painted concrete block walls, shiny polished concrete floors, stainless-steel sinks and toilets and a long wooden bench to sit or sleep on. I was placed in cell block one. They didn't lock the cage, but they did close the door behind me.

"Sorry, kid, these are the rules," they said, trying to console me because clearly the look on my face told them I wasn't loving this.

I didn't cry. I think instinctively I knew you never let anyone see you shed a tear in the slammer.

I was behind bars for about 15 minutes before a

really nice cop came and got me. He was a tall, dark-haired, Italian-looking officer.

He said, "Come on in the office with me; you don't need to be back there."

My hero.

The officer sat me down next to his desk, and we chatted for a good long while. He asked how I got all the way over to Whitehall. He was dumbfounded by my story. Hell I couldn't believe it myself, come to think of it.

As we waited for my caseworker to come and take me back to McIntyre Shelter, I noticed a policeman's hat on the desk with two holes cut in the top. I asked about the holes in the hat.

"The holes are there because they put fake bunny ears through them to play a prank on a fellow officer."

"Are you gonna throw the hat away?" I asked.

He looked at me with a grin, then looked at the hat for a second. He picked up the hat and placed it on my head. "It's yours. You take good care of it though, okay?"

"Yes sir," I said, enjoying the feel of the oversized hat falling down over my eyebrows and bumming my nose.

The hat still had the police badge on it, right in the front. I wasn't going to say anything, because I wanted it. As that thought flashed in my head, the officer spoke.

"Wait, give me that hat real quick. I have to take that badge off."

Damn, I lost my badge!

Honestly though, I'm glad he took the badge off. I didn't want to get this officer in trouble, after he'd been so kind to me.

More Foster-Family Auditions

So I was returned to McIntyre, where everyone loved my policeman's hat.

Coming up was my new foster-family audition. It was on a farm, with about five other kids. It was a sweatshop y'all. The place was dirty, the kids were dirty, with clothes and junk scattered all over the place. They wanted me bad, to lighten the load of chores, I'm sure. I clearly remember each kid in that household approaching me, asking whether or not I was going to stay with them. Even the foster mom cornered me outside with the chickens and corn.

"So, Darren, do you like it here,?" she asked, all caramel sweet, with dirty fingernails.

I stared right into her eyes and lied. "Yes ma'am, I do. I love how everyone gets along here." Lie. "I enjoy working in the fields all day long, picking weeds out of your fields." Another lie. "The food here is plentiful and delicious." Humongous lie.

What I wanted to say to her was, "Lady, when my caseworker comes to pick me up at the end of this three-day hellfest. I want you to take a good look at my ass when I leave, 'cause it's the last thing you'll ever see of me."

My next foster-family audition was in Penn Hills Township. We orphans would talk about this kind of score often: If you were going on an audition, you always wanted a rich foster family, which was definitely rare.

This new place I was about to visit was the bomb.

No kids, middle upper-class white folks. I don't mean that to be racist, but this was the early 1980s. Back then interracial families were unheard of; black families didn't want a white kid living with them and vice versa. This new family, they wanted me; trust me, I was adorable. I gave Bobby Brady from the *Brady Bunch* a run for his money on cuteness. But at the same time I must have freaked them out, because I smoked. Here I was, 13 years old, but I looked 8 years old. I'd had a baby face all my life. It was a blessing and a curse. The prospective foster dad had a woodshop in the garage. His hobby was carving people's names out of wood, and he had good skills.

He said to me during that visit, "Do you like my woodshop and that Harley-Davidson motorcycle over there in the corner? This will all be yours when I'm too old to use it."

It sounded too good to be true. The weekend went well, except for the last night of my stay. On that last night, I pissed the bed. Completely embarrassed at 3 in the morning, I carried the wet sheets down into the basement, and threw them in the dryer. After 15 long minutes, they were dry again.

One week later, in our scheduled court room, my caseworker, the rich foster family from Penn Hills Township and I were all together, waiting to make our transition into a real family. The judge came out, we all rose; then he sat and we sat.

The judge asked me if I wanted to live with them.

I said "No," stunning the whole courtroom.

The reason I turned them down was I didn't feel worthy of their kind. I left that courtroom without looking anyone in the eye. I didn't want to see anyone's pain that I had caused.

On that ride back to the shelter, my caseworker asked why I turned them down.

I said it was because I secretly wanted the Hearts to take me back. I said nothing about the pissed bed sheets, and what I just said wasn't too far from the truth.

She said, "Darren, the Hearts do not want you. You really have to come to terms with that. Plus you're getting too old for foster families. Now, I have one more family for you to visit. They've been taking in foster kids for a long time. They already have a 17-year-old foster son living with them. Just give them a chance."

Not only did I give them a chance, I stayed with them for almost a year.

Two memories come to mind with this home: I was allowed to smash glass bottles in the empty basement to release frustration; and I got it on with my new foster brother (he'd just turned 18 and I was maybe 14). We both tried to fuck each other just before bed time, but the pain was too much so we just jerked each other off. After our third time fooling around, I started feeling guilty about it, because our foster parents were really cool. They were both short, but very large individuals, who also served large meals full of love and extra potatoes. I will remember them especially fondly. My bed wetting ended at their home too, I recall.

However, I began to search for another foster home on my own.

On the school bus, a classmate befriended me after he heard I was a foster kid. He said, "I'm a foster kid, too; you should meet my foster parents."

A week later, I ran away from the foster family I was living with, to my new friend's foster home. The only thing I chose to remember about this home was there were too many kids, and in my heart I could feel the mom didn't love me. Besides, I was tired of giving the dad midnight backrubs while watching Cinemax. I had to get out of there.

Back Home Again

I made history by being the first kid to ever run away back *to* McIntyre Shelter. I didn't care. I was home again.

The following week, tragedy struck. My Grandma Dobis committed suicide by overdosing on sleeping pills. I later learned she had threatened suicide many times, asking my aunt and uncle (whom I barely knew) to come over and keep her company or she'd kill herself. Well, she finally did it. I don't mean to sound coy over this because at the time it was hard to handle.

My brothers came to McIntyre to pick me up for the funeral. My sister Lisa was at summer camp so she was unable to come; that had always saddened me. The ride to the funeral was fun for me, though, because Billy, Ricky and I were together at last. They were snorting coke and wouldn't share any with me; they said I was too young, but I was allowed to puff on a joint. This wasn't my first puff. Years earlier, when I lived with the Hearts, I went on a rare day trip with my brothers and my sister to a football field to play football together. I was 11. We all smoked a joint in the car before we got there, then Lisa and I got the giggles and didn't stop laughing for what seemed like hours.

We pulled up to the funeral home. Billy and Ricky spotted Mummy way across the street on the North Side. She was sitting on a small hill on the ground in the park, wearing a rainbow-checkered shawl, holding a brown paper bag with a beer bottle in it.

I hollered, "Mummy!"

She didn't budge or blink an eye. She may have been there on that hill, but her mind wasn't. Decades later, Mummy would reveal that she had been told she wasn't welcome in the funeral home, so she waited 'til everyone left and snuck in to take a peek at her mum. She said she hated the way Grandma looked in the casket, she didn't think it was her mum.

After the funeral we all – there was a lot of family members – gathered at our Aunt Dolly's, whom I didn't know well. But, boy, was she an Elvis Presley fanatic! Her whole house was covered in Elvis paraphernalia, clocks, lamps, dishes, throw rugs, pictures galore – every room in her house, covered in Elvis. She even named two of her four kids Elvis and Priscilla. Honest! And my sister's name? Lisa Marie – you know, after Elvis and Priscilla's daughter. Secretly I think Mummy did that on purpose so Aunt Dolly couldn't have that name to use.

Almost 10 years later I learned Aunt Dolly's boy Elvis was shot dead over a deal gone bad. Then her other son killed himself. May they rest in peace.

In that awful house, the day of Grandma's funeral was the one and only time I ever saw my brother Ricky cry. I hated being in that house with all of those family members. I was old enough to know they all sucked for not helping our family out when we truly needed it. Plus, my cousins must have stolen Billy's cocaine from his car that afternoon. My brothers thought it was me – but it wasn't. I didn't want that stuff. Not yet. Grandma Dobis, may you rest in peace.

When the day was over, I was driven back to the shelter.

Soon afterward, my caseworker approached me.

"Darren," she said, "I'm forced to tell you the bad news: We have to start finding you a group home to live in."

Oh brother, I thought. *What the hell's a group home?*
I would soon find out.

Out of the Shelter... and Into a Group Home

It wasn't long before I entered my first group home, Mars Presbyterian Home for Children, located in Mars, Pennsylvania. This place was beautiful! A humungous Tudor-style mansion on top of a flat hill, it sat on more than 10 acres and had a small swimming pool in the backyard, a tennis court and a small gymnasium in the bottom end of the mansion. Down the hill were a pair of two-story cottages. One for the girls, the other for the boys, for the older kids who had "graduated" from the mansion.

I loved living in this mansion, because I made it my very own. It had an L-shaped hallway; one side for the boys, the other for the girls. In the middle was an office for the staff to congregate and where medicine was passed out for the kids who were a little more touched than the rest of us.

This group home was run on a point system. Each of us started each day with 200 points. And whenever we misbehaved, they deducted points. At the end of the day, depending on how many points were left, you'd either be sent to bed early or you'd get a dessert treat before bed. I was sent to bed early a lot at first. I lived in the mansion with about 15 other kids. We'd band together as brothers and sisters. It was us against the staff members, or so it would seem.

When I first got to the mansion, I shared a room with this kid who was touched. A tall, thin white kid, with thick pop-bottle glasses. He walked around wearing headphones all day and night. This was back when Walkman headphones were just out. He would stand in the middle of our bedroom and bounce up and down for hours. Yes, hours!

He was on meds; and when no one was looking, he was also downing at least 12 cups of coffee a day. How did I know this? He confided in me once, in one of the few conversations we ever had. He said the private school he was taken to each day let him consume as much coffee as he wanted.

He laughed like a sinister crook when he said this. Then he put his headphones back on and began bobbing up and down on each leg, like always. Left right, left right, left right, left right. Like the letter X would look like if were bouncing. It did look somewhat therapeutic.

We kids really did form strong bonds with each other in that mansion. When we were good we would get rewarded with movie trips, and trips to the local mall. This was fun but, honestly it was embarrassing at first. I always felt like all eyes were on us when we were paraded out into society. Here we were, a mixed group of misfits. Different races, all different sizes, different mental illnesses. Clearly different. But that sense of embarrassment wouldn't last long; it quickly turned into an urge to defend my merry band of siblings. I would find myself giving any outsider the stink eye if I saw them looking at us strange, and they did – believe me, they all did.

My favorite outing event was touring the local open-house mansions that were being built in the rich neighborhoods. Now this was a sight to behold. Here these realtors were, holding their open houses, and here we come, all 15 of us. Preloaded in an extra-large white van. The counselor, Bill, who took us on these adventures, would tell us all to be respectful and not to touch anything. Yeah, right, Bill!

Actually, we were good. I made it into a daydreaming moment. I would dream that these days of being an orphan would fade away and I'd be hanging my clothes up in these football field-size closets, and I would fill up the spa tub on the second floor to lie in and relax. Oh, and could you please tell all these strange kids to get the hell out of my home?

I really did dream that in every house we toured; and yes, I tried out every upstairs tub we visited.

My New Heroes

I would live in this big, beautiful children's group-home mansion for about a year, taking forever to learn how to earn all my 200 points per day. It came mostly from maturing and greatly because of two special ladies on the Mars Group Home grounds, Miss Walker and Mrs. Barr. These ladies were my heroes.

Miss Walker was the grounds teacher and Mrs. Barr was her assistant. The school was a brand-new trailer home converted into a schoolhouse just below the mansion. It was there for the kids who couldn't quite cut it across the street at Mars High School – yup, that included me. Oh I'd been at the school, but not for long, only until I got caught smoking in the bathroom with a new friend Tom.

Next day, Tom blew his brains out with his dad's shotgun. I was supposed to have had a sleepover with him, too. I remember Tom talked badly about his dad, said he was a dick.

After that, I was sent to the on-grounds school trailer, and there they were, my heroes. Mrs. Barr was a tall lady with short curly soft brown hair, and a few gray ones starting to show. Soft spoken, she loved to tell stories about her family, and especially about her husband. He did this, he built that, she was obviously surrounded by Love, and then she would bring all that Love to us kids every day.

I miss her hugs. She reminded me of Mrs. Garrett from the TV show *Facts of Life*. Really loving. Just what the doctor ordered.

Miss Walker reminded me of a cross between Thelma from the *Scooby Doo* cartoons and a little bit of the Cathy cartoon from the Sunday newspaper. Is she still in the cartoon mix? Miss Walker had two personalities. The first was that of a stern schoolteacher who possessed the largest heart in the world. She had to; she was a schoolteacher who had to teach fuck-ups who didn't want to learn a damn thing. The other side of her personality would show up when you were one on one with her. She'd look you right in the eye and cry with you if it was called for. She loved to laugh, and I loved trying to make her laugh with a joke or a smart-ass answer.

For the majority of the time, all was calm in that classroom, but now and then an atom bomb would go off. A kid may have gotten turned down to go home, so he or she would lash out at the teachers and our class, so Miss Walker and Mrs. Barr would have to pounce on top of them and restrain them from hurting themselves or others. "Themselves" was usually the case. I lived with a bunch of suicidal kids.

Anyhow, I loved my ladies and our small classroom of five students. The curriculum was still like 3rd or 4th grade, which I liked, but now here's the gem of gems as to why this classroom worked. Miss Walker had learned a new experimental therapy called relaxation meditation. For 15 minutes she'd play a tape recording of soothing nature sounds with a calming voice that spoke, giving instruction on how to release negative energy from our bodies. Miss Walker had us lie on our backs, she'd turn the lights down. A man's voice on the recording asked us to concentrate on our toes, take in a deep breath, hold that breath in, then let the negative energy out of our toes with an exhale. Next he called out to both feet, then the knees, all the way up to the brain. Now the genius to this is, by the time you get to releasing negative energy from your head (which, by the way, is a shitload), you've already been at practice starting with your toes. Just genius.

We five kids took those lessons we learned up to the mansion to share with the other kids. It helped so much! Soon afterward, I was ready to graduate to the boys' cottage down the hill.

The days in the mansion will stay with me always. I want to acknowledge my personal counselor, Tony, who was appointed to me when I first got to the mansion. He was a short, super-muscular redheaded guy with curly, thinning hair, and thin gold wire-rimmed glasses. He had a kind soul. His job was to counsel me once a week, to see how I was doing and how was I improving behavior wise.

Toward the end of my stay at the mansion, Tony gave me thick college books on human behavior, and he made me read them. He also gave me a dictionary to look up the words I didn't know. He even once took me on a visit to my old street, Dallett Road. I wanted one last visit to my old neighborhood. The only neighbors who would let me in were little Kelly's parents, unbelievably. But when I went to visit, Kelly wasn't there, at least not in the TV room where we visited. But her parents and my bully Ricky were, they Loved him like a son.

They got to see my new look: My hair was sprayed straight up on one side, both my ears were pierced and I was smoking right in front of them. That visit was short, yet heartfelt. I'm sure they had a good old laugh when we left to go back to the mansion.

I remember one time we had an afternoon dance recital for the elderly ladies who funded the group home. They were stinking rich, I heard, and we thanked God for that. At the outdoor dance recital, I befriended a news anchor named Jon Burnett, who worked for KDKA TV. And – you know it – I wanted to go live with him and his family. He bragged about them so much I got jealous.

I didn't ask him to take me home. I just sat there and listened like an orphan with a desperate family-longing crush. One other thing about Jon. I once took him to lunch while I was homeless. I never mentioned to him I was homeless during our lunch; and no, I didn't ask him to take me home that time, either. Then, at the end of our lunch, he paid the bill.

It'll be my turn next time, Jon.

On a sad, scarier note, we kids messed up real bad on this one kid. Yeah the kid took meds, and the kid was a bit of a twirl. This kid could be super sweet one minute, and get way turned out the next. After dinner once, for some reason we started calling the kid a spaz, tauntingly. Back then that was a word you yourself never wanted to be called, as it implied you were crazy. But we did it anyway, and with gusto. But it backfired quickly. The kid began furiously stabbing himself in the hand with a fork – and the blood was everywhere! We shut up real fast, but the damage was already done.

I ran to the office to tell on the kid, and not us horrible instigators. The staff raced up to the dining room and tried to calm the kid down. They needed four staff members to restrain him and carry this broken soul downstairs to what was called the "break room." It was a small, padded light-green room with a punching bag hanging in the corner, awaiting tiny fists of fury.

I apologized to the kid the next day and we hugged like it never happened. Years later, I learned he landed in jail for slamming a baby up against a brick wall. To this day I'm still sorry about that ever happening. I knew better than that. I'm a Lover, not a fighter, but I wasn't that sad night.

Life Down the Hill

Time to move, time to leave my mansion. Down the hill I went, to the boys' cottage. This place I would compare to a fraternity house, with two staff security guards on duty 24/7. I still attended the on-grounds school trailer, but we were let out early this one day because the Space Shuttle Challenger had blown up. It was the one with the school-teacher, Christa McAuliffe, on it. Later that night, a staff member came up to me, making a joke about that tragedy. He asked me "What was the last question the teacher on the shuttle asked?"

"What?"

He said, "She asked, 'What's this red button do?'"

These were the kind of people I was surrounded by. I couldn't escape. Well, actually, I *could* have, because we weren't on lockdown. The door was wide open; you could run if you wanted to. But I never did.

At this time in my life I was learning the new music and loving its entrance into the world for the first time… at least to me. One of my orphan brothers introduced us on his double-cassette boom box. Rap Music's her name, spittin' lyrics is her game. Run DMC was the hottest sound out there at the time, but we had to listen to them on cassette tapes because the radio wasn't playing their songs yet. Doug E. Fresh was the freshest rapper.

I also remember at that time I faked failing an eye exam just so I could get a pair of glasses. I picked out a pair of those big Sally Jesse Raphael round brown tortoiseshell ones.

Two memories of the cottage home would follow me throughout my life. The first one involved my friend Michael Clark. He didn't live at the cottage; he was an old friend, a year younger than me, I think. We met back when I lived with the Hearts. He was also my first homosexual experience.

I had stolen a *Penthouse* magazine from Mr. Heart and brought it to Michael's house for a sleepover. After we read a few forum letters, we began to wrestle around, eventually landing on the floor, naked, in a 69 position. We sucked each other off.

Afterward, I asked him if he had ever done that before.

"Sure," he said casually, then rattled off the names of six other boys we went to school with – they were all the jocks and the popular boys from our seventh-grade class.

This pissed me off because I knew these kids he named were making fun of him behind his back, calling him a fag. But I, too, fell prey to the art of homosexual embarrassment, and its guilty love.

After that night, I ignored him in the school hallways for the next three days. Then I went back to his place for another sleepover.

Several years later, while I lived at the cottage, a letter came in the mail for me. It was from Michael Clark. No one had ever reached out to me from a former foster home or group home; no one but Michael, that is.

The protocol for receiving letters in a children's group home is that you have to open them in front of a staff member. As I unfolded the letter, a pornographic playing card fell into my lap, a close-up picture of a big-dicked guy fucking this lady's pussy. Thank God the staff member in the office was busy talking on the phone, because I was able to shove that card into my pocket without him noticing. I finished opening the letter, showing there weren't drugs or porno cards in it, and off I went.

At the end of his seven-page letter, Michael asked, "What do you think of the playing card I sent? That guy's got a big one."

The second lasting memory of that boys' cottage is what I suspect got me kicked out of the cottage. It was when I was 15 and coerced an older kid to fool around.

Within a week, I was shown to two different group homes for older kids. These places were geared toward getting 18-year-old orphans ready for independent adult living. You know, when the government's done footing the bill.

One group home was named Whales Tails. I stayed with them for a trial period. I didn't like it there; they were too strict, as I recall. Then came Abraxas Young Adult Group Home. After that weekend visit, I coined a new term to describe it to my caseworker.

"That place was cherry," I said.

"Cherry?" she asked. "What does that mean?"

I said, "It's my most favorite-flavor pie, cherry. That group home was cherry."

Before I knew it, I was moved in, living with young adults. I was only 15; I really shouldn't have been there to begin with. Too late.

Growing Up... in a Hurry

My Abraxas home – what a place this was! I was the youngest of about 10 of us. The building we lived in was a three-story white house, third house down from the street corner, on the East Side of Pittsburgh, in the middle of a regular neighborhood. This to me was weird, a group home in a neighborhood. Bizarre. I always figured the neighbors must have hated having 10 kids living next to them. But that's how it was. The vibe at this home was a relaxed environment, a really laid-back feel.

On my first day there, two older kids approached me. The taller one had short dark hair, thin beady brown eyes, and an unshakeable white-trash swagger. I say it that way, 'cause it takes one to know one. The other kid had super-curly orange-blond hair, and that same swagger. They were both slender; in fact, they really reminded me of *Beavis and Butthead*, the MTV cartoon back in the '90s.

They once tried hitting on me with their dicks hard under their underpants. A dick can't lie – but I had this funny feeling if I'd touched their big penises, they were gonna punch me. So I didn't. Never.

Beavis and Butthead approached me up on the third floor, where my bedroom was. The three of us had different bedrooms on that floor, plus a shared living area. That's where they told me their story.

Beavis asked if I'd heard about the two kids who got caught breaking into the Pittsburgh Zoo and torturing the flamingos by tearing off their legs.

The second he said this, I turned away from them so my face wouldn't reveal the disgust and resentment that began swelling up in me, because I knew what was coming next. He was going to confess his sins to me, and I had nowhere to hide. Time for some damn good acting.

"Yeah," I said as nonchalantly as I could.

Beavis stared at me. "We did it." He sounded proud.

I gave them my full attention, eye to eye. "Are you kidding me?" I knew this was nothing to kid about.

"Yup," Butthead said, beginning to snicker like a successful bank robber.

"Wow. Wow!" I couldn't stop that word coming out of my mouth. "Wow." I ended it with a question. "Why did you do it?"

Beavis shrugged. "'Cause I wanted to see if they could fly without their legs."

"Did they?" I asked.

"Nope," Butthead piped up.

Now I was scared shitless. I'd just learned I was sharing the third floor of this group home with two of the most-hated kids in all of Pittsburgh! And again I've got nowhere to hide.

At that point, someone must have hollered, "Dinner!"

Thank God for that! We all scrambled downstairs to the second floor to eat and the subject was never brought up again... but who could forget it?! I never knew whether they were just messing with me or if they actually tortured those poor birds. Honestly, why anyone would even want to claim that story as their own is a mystery to me.

Because this was a group home for kids preparing to get out on their own, we kids did all the housework, cleaning up, laundry and cooking. The staff weren't our maids anymore; we had to learn to do everything on our own, which made sense. When trouble did occur, like if someone ran away, the staff devised a system that involved the fellow kids to deal with it.

Whoever ran away had to stand in the middle of the living room while three randomly picked kids would confront the offender. They'd reprimand him and explain why he shouldn't have run off (or done whatever else it was he did), and how much we loved him and how much it hurt when he was gone.

This would usually end with everyone crying and hugging; then the three kids would have to come up with the other kid's punishment. That was awesome, because the punishments were always light.

I wasn't picked to reprimand anyone until a month or two after I moved in. I was the new guy and didn't know anyone that well yet; plus, I was really quiet and shy.

But when the time came, I blew up loudly – and how! I can't remember the name of the kid we were yelling at, but I remember being allowed to scream and cry out loud. It was a chance for me to release the pain I was holding onto within myself. At least, that's how I viewed it. Everyone was in shock that I was so boisterous... and frankly, so was I.

Peabody High School

At Abraxas, if you weren't in school anymore, you were required to get a job. I was enrolled in Peabody High School in East Liberty. Today it is named, Pittsburgh Obama of International Studies. They put me in the ninth grade. I knew I couldn't keep up with the other students academically, but I didn't say anything because I figured they would figure it out eventually.

This school and the neighborhood were predominantly black, but one morning I noticed this white girl walking with friends toward the school. She looked really familiar. Then I recognized her. She was my foster cousin, Michele, from when I lived with Mr. and Mrs. Heart. She recognized me too, as we'd spent many holiday gatherings together. But this wasn't *her* neighborhood, either.

"What are *you* doing here?" we asked each other simultaneously.

I told her my story, and she said her parents had separated. We hugged but we barely saw each other after that. I wanted us to be friends but she had changed; she wasn't the bubbly little girl I grew up with anymore.

I have two distinct memories of Peabody High. One is of a small, skinny old black teacher who befriended me. He had one ear pierced and he wore a small gold hoop earring, which was practically unheard of back then, especially for an old dude. He took me to his place once after school, and asked if I wanted to make some money. He said I could clean his stove for him for a few bucks.

I did, but not before he showed me black-and-white pictures of his dead white boyfriend. I had thought this guy was gay. He even showed me some old-time gay porn; but, weirdly (I thought), he didn't hit on me.

Instead, he said, "I gotta go to the store. I'll be right back."

Meanwhile, I cleaned the stove; it only took about two seconds. All he had me do really was replace the tin foil on the burners with new tin foil. After that, all that was left for me to do was to go in his bedroom and jerk off with the old black-and-white gay porn pictures.

He was gone for what seemed like forever, but I suspect he had walked around the back and was spying on me through the window. It was pitch dark outside, so he easily could have been.

When I was finished, he came back, then took me back home to Abraxas. We never spoke in school after that.

My second Peabody memory was of a poster I saw in the hallway, asking students to sign up for an eight-week modern-dance summer class at a dance studio at the Pittsburgh Carnegie Museum. I was all in, because it gave me somewhere to go during the summer; and I got to be on stage.

The last time I'd been on stage was while I lived with the Hearts. I had entered the school talent show with Diane from down the street. We made up a dance routine to the song "Fame" by Irene Cara.

At the end of our well-received performance, I remember running, all by myself, down this empty hallway, where the lights were dim. I danced and skipped, hands in the air, and thanked God for letting me get on stage.

So now to be in another dance performance was awesome. I learned a new word, too: *Professional.* I had to buy soft dance shoes, black leotards, because that's what the guys wore, and show up on time. Which I did, because I loved it.

I was given permission by the Abraxas Children's Independence Center to take the bus down to the dance studios, which in itself was awesome. In the dance studio, there were several instructors; they were their own dance company called Alloy. They were helping underprivileged youth receive a dance-class opportunity. I think I was the only boy out of eight of us kids.

At the end of the second class, one of the male instructors came up to me and said, "You don't know this because you just don't know about this yet, but guys in leotards have to wear a cup over their groin."

Thank God for him, because I was a bit embarrassed, because in the gay world lingo, I was a grow-er not a show-er. And yes, the girls were looking and giggling. Bitches. Ahh, I'm only kidding, we had a lot of fun with each other in that class.

We rehearsed all summer long.

Then show time came and we were staged behind the museum in the backyard courtyard, on these extremely long stretched-out stairs, which acted as our stage. But when it came time for the big performance, no one from Abraxas came to see me perform. Not a staff member, not even one brother. This was a wake-up call for me. They weren't my brothers, they were out for themselves. Hell, we all were.

After that happened I started to become more independent and wanted another way to get out of the Abraxas home – not to run away, just to get out of there. That place was crawling with unusual characters.

This one girl wore a bandana 24/7, and she was a Cyndi Lauper fanatic, just like me. So one afternoon, while listening to Cyndi Lauper's *True Colors* album on cassette, she shared with me why she wore bandanas all the time. She took her bandana off to reveal bald splotches all over her scalp. She had a bad habit of pulling her hair out – without knowing it. Then she did it right in front of me. She put her fingers real close to her head, twirled a few strands of hair around her fingers and just plucked them out like she was pulling weeds out of a garden.

These other two kids – a beautiful long-haired blonde girl and her blond goatee-sporting hippie guy – were dating and running away, often every other weekend, to do heroin. She was six months pregnant. It seemed like a lot of the girls at Abraxas were pregnant.

Learning About the Real World... Working, Hangovers and Independent Living

My very first job was working for McDonald's when I was just 15. It was legal, provided the folks at Abraxas gave me permission.

As a cashier, I learned to greet customers with a smile, give them their exact change back and at the end of my shift, pocket the extra cash in the drawer. This was done by not pushing the buttons on the register to indicate a sale.

I worked there for almost two months, I got really good with math... until I got fired. Oh, I didn't get fired for stealing. I figured out I could cruise downtown instead of going to work, and my group home wouldn't suspect a thing. That was, until my boss called them up and busted me.

One Fourth of July, Abraxas loaded us up in the van to go downtown to watch the fireworks at Point Park, where three rivers meet up. The Monongahela and the Allegheny rivers join together, then turn into the Ohio River. At "the Point" there's a fountain they turn on in the summertime. The fountain looks like it shoots 50 feet in the air. It's beautiful.

We were allowed to split up into groups and meet back up at a designated time and place. I was paired up with Beavis and Butthead, who took me to a liquor store and introduced me to Miss Tiger Rose wine. She was red-dish purple in color, and tasted good. Well, by the third swig she tasted good. Until the ride home, when she came back to visit in the form of vomit. Out the side of the van, going 35 miles an hour. They opened side door and held onto me while Miss Tiger Rose left me for the speeding concrete below.

Next morning I experienced my first full-blown hangover. Then I had to wash the puke off the van, inside and out. It was gross.

To teach the kids who lived at Abraxas how to live independently, the center rented apartments around the neighborhood. Somehow I was given permission to move into a second-floor apartment up the street, on the corner of South Negley Ave. and Friendship Ave. My bedroom was a round corner room with a large curved window overlooking the street lights.

That's where I lost my virginity to a girl August 30. I remember like it was yesterday. It was my 16th birthday and I didn't want to be a virgin with a girl anymore.

My first attempt at losing my virginity had been three years earlier, on one of my runaway adventures. It was in the attic of our rescuers from the streets – four tall, kindhearted black guys in their early 20s.

They took me in, along with these two girls my age. Lynn, this girl I knew from school, who had beautiful, long red hair, was a wild child like me. The other girl was beautifully black, with smooth dark skin. They let us stay there for two weeks free, room and board and spaghetti sandwiches (that's spaghetti on a loaf of white bread) every night, no kidding, every single night. I couldn't figure out why they were allowing us to stay with them free. That is, 'til at the end of the second week when I walked in on the black girl getting gang banged by all four guys. She looked like she was having fun.

One of the guys saw me and yelled, "Hey, get over here and get you some of dis."

That's when kindness showed up. The girl told the guys to leave the attic, they did. Then she let me dry hump her for what seemed an eternity, but I'm sure it was only

30 seconds.

She reached down between us to confirm my limp dick, and whispered, "It's okay, I won't tell anyone about this."

I snuck away from that house by myself early the next morning.

But now it's my 16th birthday. What the hell, let's say there was a full moon, too (there was, actually).

Around dinnertime we realized there were no staff members on duty. So we went wild. I got drunk and let this little pudgy white girl seduce me in my second-story round bedroom. She gave me head. I was limp at first, but then I closed my eyes and pretended not to be with her.

The moment I was hard she laid back and said, "Stick it in there." She was a real classy chick, a real pro, huh? My first time, but definitely not hers.

An hour later I would lose my virginity a second time, getting fucked by a gay neighbor I'd befriended months earlier. He used to let me come over and look at his porn collection. He would try to hit on me but I wasn't having it… yet. He was this tall, skinny half-Chinese, half-black guy with the biggest condom-covered dick ever. He bent over me but when he saw me crying from the pain, he stopped.

But that pain was nothing compared to what was about to happen in the next two days.

Going Home?

I'd gotten called to the principal's office at Peabody High, but instead of going there, I caught a bus and headed for downtown Pittsburgh. This had become a regular trip for me by now so I really thought nothing of it. It was a warm, sunny day and I was running out of hair spray.

So off to Woolworths I went. Stealing from them was easy, until I headed toward the exit sign with a large pink can of Aqua Net Extra Hold under my coat.

Suddenly there came a 180-degree spin forced on me by security. This was a first for me and I didn't like it. Plus the dude had the tightest grip on my arm I'd ever felt. I wasn't going anywhere.

He took me into the office. I sat in the interrogation chair, answering who I was and where was I from. Then a police officer showed up. I was getting really scared.

To my surprise, the store security guy said they weren't going to press charges.

"Son," the cop said. I really liked that he called me that. "We're gonna call your group home to come get you, because we haven't got time to take you back."

Yeah, so what? I thought. *Whatever.*

So the security guard got Abraxas on the phone. "Hello. Yes, ma'am, we have a Darren Timothy Numer down here at our store, we caught him stealing. We're not going to press charges but can you come down here and pick him up?" He paused and said, "Okay," then hung up the phone.

He looked at me and said, "They don't want you back."

It felt like I'd been kicked in the gut. I couldn't believe what I had heard. They didn't want me back. It was like the Hearts all over again.

They even called McIntyre Shelter, but they turned me away, too.

The policeman asked me, "Do you have a relative that can pick you up?"

My world went deafeningly quiet. I was knocked the fuck out. I couldn't stop repeating their question in my head. *Do you have a relative that can pick you up? Do you have a relative that can pick you up? Do you have a relative that can pick you up?*

Hell no, I ain't got no fucking relative that can pick me up, not fucking one, you all know that, I thought. Then the cop broke up the madness stirring around in my head.

"Do you maybe have an older brother who could come get ya?"

Brother? I thought. *Yes.* "Yes, I do," I replied.

It was truly a long shot, but I gave the officers Billy's telephone number. Amazingly, he answered.

After they hung up the phone, they told me, "He'll be here in a half hour."

After 16 long years I was going home. I didn't cry tears of joy in front of anyone, but I could have. I honestly could have. I was going home! I was finally fuckin' going home!

Billy, my eldest brother, was a highly skilled carpenter. He looked like John Travolta and he and his friends partied like rock stars. At that point in my life, he was the king of my world, because we didn't get to grow up together. That, I believe is why, whenever we were together, he was really intense with teaching me about the world. Billy would school me on people's behavior and how to deal with them.

He once told me, "When you learn how to drive, Darren, stay in the slow lane, and stay stress free. Screw the speed demons, they're definitely gonna get a ticket. Why would you wanna do something stupid like that?"

Then he'd say, "And stay out of fist fights; they're the dumbest things on earth. Learn to talk your way out of a fight. That's the only way – only way both parties can ever win."

That one I took to heart fully.

Waiting that half hour for my brother Billy was the fastest half hour I ever waited. He drove up in someone else's small beat-up truck, not his usual pristine 1984 black Monte Carlo with light-tan cloth interior. The bench seats were covered with a white bed sheet with tiny burn holes in it. We hugged on the sidewalk, got in the truck and got the hell out of there.

"What did you get caught stealing, Darren?" Billy asked.

When I told him hair spray, he gave me the strangest look, as if I were pushing on a door that clearly states "Pull."

"What the hell you need that for?"

I didn't answer.

"Look," he said when we reached the house, "I got a few friends over. You ain't telling them you stole hair spray. Say 'tennis shoes' instead. Oh, yeah, Ricky's coming over, too."

Yahoo! I screamed internally, ignoring my brother's command.

If you'd ever met my brother Ricky, you would've screamed "Yahoo!" too. He had that effect on people. Everyone loved Ricky Numer... that is, if he let you. He's the second oldest of us; Lisa's younger and I'm the baby.

I would compare Ricky to a wise old owl high up in a tree. You have to look for him; he won't make himself known to you. He was taller than me, little on the thin side, but strong as an ox. He loved to arm wrestle me each time he saw me. After he defeated me every time, he'd pound once on his chest and say, "You feel me?"

He hated heartless educated people. And don't shake his hand unless you want your hand broken. That handshake was always in for the kill. Years later I would only ever hug him. Screw that handshake.

Ricky wasn't book smart; he couldn't have been. He was always on the run from one foster family and then another. The foster dads loved his big dick. He once told me he got hit on all the time. Ricky hung out with the wild children of the night. He was never an instigator to fight, but he never backed down from one either. He had beautiful dark-blond short hair that he slicked back with baby oil.

In that short white truck, Billy and I pulled up to his grandma's house – the old Victorian. Inside, three of Billy's friends were sitting around the coffee table strewn with cocaine, marijuana and Iron City beer.

"Want a beer, kid?" one of Billy's friends asked.

"Sure, thanks."

As he tossed it in the air to me, he asked, "So, what'd they bust you for?"

Billy answered for me. "Tennis shoes. Damn, Darren, I thought I taught you better than that. Never steal anything if they're watching ya. Didn't you see them watching ya?"

I didn't say a word.

"Go into the kitchen and get yourself something to eat," Billy said.

While I was in the kitchen, I heard Ricky come through the door. I ran so fast to him and we embraced for what seemed like forever and we didn't care who was looking.

Then we kissed right on the lips. Nothing sexual. But it was from years of having those damn short family visits. That was just how much we Loved each other. We all really Loved each other so much. Every time we'd get back together, a Bible verse would go through my head, something saying, 'Always greet thy brother with a Holy kiss.' So we did, still do to this day. We greet each other that way. Mummy taught us that kiss.

Later that night, we smoked a joint laced with coke. I still wasn't allowed to snort coke, but I did get to smoke two puffs.

Twenty minutes later I asked Billy if I could go upstairs and listen to his records. They were all watching boring football on TV, but upstairs Billy had a kick-ass sound system. He said yes, but because the drugs were kicking in I couldn't stand up. I crawled up the Victorian staircase, causing everyone in the living room to howl with laughter.

"Shut the fuck up!" I told them scornfully, which only made them laugh even louder. I was hoping for that. Billy had really cute guy friends, but I was nowhere near ready to tell him that. Though I did suspect Ricky had an idea that I was gay.

Upstairs I felt like I was floating in the air, listening to The Jackson 5 *Victory* album with thick headphones on. The song I was listening to was called "Always." This to me was the most beautiful song I had ever felt, while listening to it for the very first time, the drugs were playing their part too. But I was knocked down when Ricky came into the dark room I was in, and began to wrestle a little bit with me.

He held me close to him and ask me, "How you doing, brother?" He would always call me that, we all did to each other. "You doing okay?"

"Yeah I'm okay," I said.

"Why don't you get some rest? Sounds like you had a long day."

A Rude Awakening

I woke up Saturday morning with the headphones still on. The smell of bacon and eggs had made their way upstairs. So I followed the smells back down the staircase. The morning sun lit up the clean living room – not a trace of last night's festival. Both my brothers are immaculate house cleaners, unlike me. Grandma Numer had left for work and Billy had the day off. Ricky, the roofer, didn't. He was already gone. Which was good, because I had a question to lay on the table with my eldest brother.

Breakfast was over, I took a shower, put on fresh clean clothes. I walked into the living room and straight-out asked Billy if I could live with him and Grandma.

"I don't think Grandma could handle you, Darren. I'm sorry, she's too old to raise another kid."

I shook my head. "Don't say another word, Billy. I completely understand," I lied.

I was crushed. Time to run and hide again.

"Hey, I'm out of smokes," I said, trying to sound nonchalant. "I'm gonna go pick up a pack. Isn't there a 7-Eleven around the corner?"

"Yeah, three blocks down. Do you need some cash?"

The second he asked that, I knew our relationship was if not over, then definitely changed.

In my mind, that cash was goodbye money. I put on my coat really slowly, to give him time to change his mind about my staying. That didn't happen, I grabbed the cash and the door handle, opened the door and exited.

When I was about 50 feet away from the house I started to cry and talk to God. "Well, I guess this is it, God, Dad," I would call him through a forced adoption I placed on him since I didn't have a real father.

Then the voice showed up again. It said, "Just keep walking, and don't you turn around to look back for your brother. I have separated you two. There's more for you to learn."

I began to cry harder, and yup I turned around to look for Billy.

Then I heard, "Yes, he's looking for you; but he will not find you."

For some reason I always knew deep down inside this was going to happen. I was now, officially, homeless.

Homeless

The little money I'd had in my pocket had to last, and for what? The fuck if I knew! I'm homeless – mother-fucking homeless. When you've never been homeless, you never miss or think about your bed, or even the pillow on your bed. You never think about the glasses and dishes in the kitchen cabinets. You never miss the front door of your home. But you miss the fuck out of them the second you become homeless.

I was fucking homeless. And I was trying my hardest not to cry, but failing big time. Oh, God, such an empty feeling that was!

There are no colors I can choose to describe this feeling. It's odorless, weightless and ear-to-ear numbing. But I had to stop crying on the sidewalk.

Ya gotta buck up, ya don't wanna attract unwanted attention of any passersby. So guess who pops into my head at that moment? Petula Clark's 1965 hit song, "Downtown."

Guess where I went: As Petula sang, "Things'll be great when you're…" That's right – Downtown!

Downtown Pittsburgh! Holy goodness, here I come, old friend. Looks like we'll be bunking together for awhile. Time to get our hustle on.

I'd get there by bus, buy a pack of smokes and be dead broke.

When living on the streets, you have the three main unstoppable forces. You get thirsty, you get hungry and you gotta take a shit. Controlling being thirsty is easy.

There are water fountains everywhere, and free water in every fast food joint – bathrooms too. But don't go too often to just one place; they'll turn you away.

Food was a bit harder to come by. There was the soup kitchen down the street somewhere. I made a personal point to never eat at a soup kitchen, ever, because I thought it would seal the deal that I was homeless; plus I didn't feel worthy of their kind.

I viewed being homeless as being the hardest job out there by far, and I wanted to quit this job fast. This job is harder than being an astronaut, doctor and a judge, combined.

So if you aren't gonna eat at soup kitchens, like me, you've got to get money somehow.

The Ten O'clock Hustle

Around 10 p.m. the streets were in slow motion. There was this tall slender street hustler I met earlier in the day on Liberty Ave., in a video arcade. That's where the pervy old men came to watch the kiddies play. We became friends when I threw a few cigarettes his way. Cigarettes are like gold on the streets; you got smokes, you got peace among friends. I always had smokes. I'd jack 'em from 7-Elevens, back when they didn't have security cameras – and before the smokes were kept behind the registers. To this day, I still feel responsible for security cameras coming out; but at the same time those security cameras actually helped break me of my kleptomania years later.

My tall probably-18-year-old new friend looked kinda like a cross between Axl Rose from Guns and Roses and Sebastian Bach, the lead singer of the band Skid Row.

"You hustle?" Axl Bach asked me, out of the blue.

"Whatchu mean?" I asked. I kinda knew what he meant, but I needed to hear it said aloud, to make it real.

"You know," A.B. said, "fuck people for money, or just let 'em blow ya." Then he said, "You're gay, right?"

"How'd you know?"

He chuckled at me and never answered. "Tell ya what," he said, "meet me across the street tonight around 10 o'clock. The arcade owner don't like us turning tricks on his property. He prefers we go across the street."

So about 10 o'clock, I was standing across from the arcade, in front of a porn shop, ironically enough.

Up walks A.B., my new, dirty, kinda-sexy hustler friend. "Gotta smoke?"

I tossed the pack at him.

He took one out and lit it, then threw the pack back.

"You can have more if you want," I suggested, trying to flirt with him.

"Naw, I'm good."

"Are you gay?" I asked.

"I'm bi, but I like girls better."

That ended my flirtations.

So then I asked, "Did you ever do it with an old lady?"

Almost laughing, A.B. replied, "Yeah. They're all wrinkly and shit, but they give great head when they take their teeth out."

I burst out laughing.

Then he said, "Look. D'you see these cars slowing down as they pass by?"

Honestly, I hadn't noticed that until he mentioned it. I knew then what I was looking at. I was produce, and these were shopping carts going by.

He said, "It's better to stand closer to the street, so they can get a good look at you. When you're standing right up against the building, that means no; you're telling them, 'Not tonight.' When they roll up, they'll turn their window down. The first thing you do is ask them, 'Are you a cop?' They have to tell you the truth, 'cause it's the law."

It wasn't, as I would learn years later.

Just at that moment, a car rolled up and A.B. said, "Stand back there. I know this guy."

He walked up to the car, they had a few words, then he jumped in the car and he was gone.

In case you don't know what just happened there, let me school you. A.B. went to turn a trick, to blow that guy, or get blown, whatever was on that guy's shopping list.

He made me stand back so the john (the guy who was driving the shopping cart) couldn't get a good look at me. I was basically competition now.

Not long afterward, a dark-blue van pulled up beside me. I was standing in the middle of the sidewalk. This nerdy 40-year-old skinny-looking creepy guy with greasy black hair and thick '50s-style black-rimmed glasses rolled down his window.

He said something to me but I put my head down and turned toward the building.

He drove around the block four times, then finally left. Next, a brown-striped sedan pulled up then took off, like a scared little bunny.

Then this kinda-handsome, middle-aged guy with short brown hair went around the block two times before pulling up.

I walked to his car as he lowered his passenger-side window. "What's up?"

"Not much," he said.

It was chilly that night, and I could feel the heat from inside his car. *Come on, dude, ask me in already, for Pete's sake, I'm freezing out here!*

"You need a ride somewhere?"

No I don't need a ride anywhere, where the hell would I gooooo—— oh, I get it now, we're still doing this other thing. "Are you a cop?" I asked. "You have to tell me, you know."

He laughed and said, "No, I'm not. Come on, get in."

So here we go. I was fixin' to turn a trick.

He said, "Boy, you're cute. You must hear that all the time."

"I don't know," I lied.

He was nice, but OMG was he touchy feely! He started petting me like a cat. My dick wasn't hard and that made me nervous, 'cause I'm thinking that's kind of an important requirement in this line of work. Then he started petting me down over my crotch. *Houston, we have lift off!*

I reached for his dick, but he pushed my hand away.

"Lay your car seat as far back as you can," he told me. "Pull your dick out. I wanna see it."

I did as he asked, pushing it to stand straight up.

"Wow, that's a big one!" he exclaimed. "Why do all you little guys have the big dicks?"

I don't know if he was joking with me, but that has to be the best compliment you can ever give a guy, that's right up there with I love you.

He went into his glove box and pulled out a small tube, squeezed out some squishy stuff in his hand and proceeded to go to town with his hot hand as he drove along the darkened streets.

Wow! I couldn't believe this was really happening.

I exploded over his hand in less than a minute. He had Kleenex in his glove box, too. He cleaned me up and I pulled up my pants.

When we returned to the pickup spot, he reached into his wallet and pulled out a twenty.

I stared straight at it and thought, *If you take it you're a whore; if you don't, you go hungry.*

"No thanks," I said to him. "I'm good; but really, thanks anyway."

"Why?" he asked with a bewildered look on his face.

I smiled. "To be honest with you, mister, you were my very first, and I like you."

He told me, "Well then, here – take the money. Consider it a gift."

I said, "No, keep your money, and you consider me your gift. Go, take good care of yourself."

We smiled at each other, I got out of the car and closed the door. He drove off, leaving me on the edge of the sidewalk to watch his taillights fade into the night.

I was pooped, so I needed to rest. I found some bushes on a five-foot wall nearby, so when no one was looking, I jumped up on top of the wall, crawled under the bushes and passed out on the hard compacted dirt. The thick bushes shielded me from the cold winds that night. *Thank you bushes, I've never forgotten you.*

Pervy Deacon

I'd been on the streets for a short time but one evening I was standing on the sidewalk – close to the street like a good little hooker boy – and who rolls up? A deacon from one of my past foster families' churches. I won't rat him out by saying which foster home it was; I'll just leave that between him and God. But did I know who he was? Damn skippy, I did.

I hopped into his car without the cop question.

The first thing out of his mouth was, "You look so familiar."

I should. You been passing out church pamphlets to me for years, I should look familiar to you. I told him who I was and who my foster mother used to be, he then remembered.

So then this tool job took me all the way to his house, which he shared with whom I can only assume was his lover. When we walked into his home, I was introduced to this big fat guy, who couldn't even be bothered to get out of his chair to say hi to me. Hell, he didn't even turn away from the TV set. I clearly wasn't the first of my kind to be in their house.

Then the deacon got on the phone and called up some old church friends of mine who were my age, and put me on the phone with them. The way he was close to them like that I can only assume he must have gotten it on with them, too.

My old friends on the phone asked me what I was doing there. I told them everything but the truth. Those friends on the phone were also friends to whose home I had ran away from McIntyre Shelter twice. Their parents were thinking about being my foster folks, but they changed their minds at the last minute. I don't blame them; their household already had two teenage boys and a Down syndrome older sister to take care of. I would have been adding too much to the equation. I even saw those boys skateboarding downtown once while I was homeless. I tried to say hi, but they ignored me. Or maybe they didn't recognize me.

After I hung up the phone, the dorky, grey-haired, goateed deacon led me downstairs to a clean, carpeted basement. He tried to kiss me, but I backed away. I wanted out of there so fast, and at the same time, I wanted him to adopt me too. Funny, huh?

He pulled down the zipper on his pants and pulled out his hard little baby garden snake-size penis.

I reached down to touch it, and he yelled at me saying, "No!" He immediately began coming on the carpet. He was visibly mad and embarrassed and I tried not to laugh.

He cleaned up and then gave me the bum's rush me out of his home. "You gotta go. Come on, let's go."

He threw a five-dollar bill in my hand, then walked me out the front door and locked me out. That asshole made me walk like seven blocks to the nearest bus stop – which was, ironically, right next to his church. But thank God the bus took me back into my city.

Many years later, I went back to that church. I went up to him at the end of the service and asked, "Do I look familiar?"

He said, "No."

I felt God button my lip, so I just laughed at him, shaking my head, and walked away.

When I made it back to Pittsburgh that night, I was still broke, so I remembered about Zack's, a gay bar I was told to go stand in front of because it was a good hookup place to make money. So I went there and was immediately attracted to it every time the door opened, because they were playing loud dance music.

I walked in, past security, past the coat check and headed straight for the dance floor. I closed my eyes and let the music take me away. A short, curly-haired, Italian-looking college guy came up and began dancing with me. He asked if he could buy me a drink.

We sat down with our drinks on one of the stair-cases of this four-story dance club, French kissing and talk-ing for about two hours. He asked me a thousand ques-tions; I gave him two thousand answers.

He couldn't believe I was homeless. When the bar was closing, he wanted to take me home with his two gay female roommates. They were all physiology majors and they wanted to rescue me from the streets. At their place, they all agreed I could live with them as long as I pulled my weight. I was their homemaker for the next two years; but most of all, I wasn't homeless anymore.

New Living Arrangements

My new roommates were incredible. There was Steven, who was 22. Robin was a beautiful, tall, skinny black 21-year-old bisexual who also had a serious kleptomania problem; but getting caught stealing a long white trench coat from Kaufmann's department store (where she worked) eventually cured her. The other roommate was Cindy, a big, bold mid-20s lesbian who I'm sure didn't really want me there to begin with, but she was outnumbered by the others. She was never mean to me, but I would catch her staring at me out of the corner of her eye all the time.

We lived in a second-floor apartment on the South Side. The entrance was around the back, up a flight of steep, scary wooden stairs – and in the wintertime it was impossible to not fall down them. I hated those stairs!

So what do you do when you take in a homeless guy as a new roommate? You throw a party! About 20 of their college friends came over to meet me. One of them was an old friend of mine, Michelle, the girl whose bathing suit top I pulled down at the Whitehall pool. That's what she said to me when we reunited. And from that moment, we were inseparable.

Michelle had her dad's credit cards, and she loved taking me out to restaurants, teaching me proper etiquette. I also remember going through a British-accent phase, too, while we were at those restaurants. I was bloody good at it until someone from England asked me where I was from. That put an end to that charade.

I used to take Michelle to the gay bars I was able to sneak into. We had a lot of fun back in those days. She taught me how to drive her dad's station wagon; because I was basically still on the run from the authorities – as an underage orphan – I couldn't get my driver's license 'til I was 18.

I had a small fender bender with that station wagon once. We blamed it on her dad because he was notorious for getting drunk and crashing his car into houses. But he was a dentist and all the local police officers loved him, so he never got into trouble. He just had to pay the bill for fixing the homes. Her dad once worked on my teeth, free. He was bald and witty, with the most wonderful wife, who allowed me to call her "Mom" from the first day we met. I Love and miss them both. Rest in peace.

We lived in that upstairs apartment on the South Side for about three months, until Steven's parents offered us one side of their duplex, in the Mt. Washington district, on Sutherland Ave. Pretty common looking for that area and, lucky me, my bedroom was in the attic.

Our new home was a fixer upper, which to this day I believe is still not fixed up. Steven's dad would come over every other weekend and try to repair this or that. He was a funny, loving old man who loved the ladies, a lot.

He once said to me, "Darren, do you know how to get a woman to fuck you?"

"No."

"You just come right out and ask them, 'Hey, you wanna fuck?' Sure you're gonna get slapped a lot. But you'll get laid sometimes, too."

Then he'd add the cutest grin you ever did see to that story. He looked just like one of those ceramic gnomes you'd see in someone's front yard. I liked him a lot. We all called him Pops.

The house was three stories high and you could break into your neighbor's side of the house by crawling through the attic's small crawlspace. Go ahead, ask me how

I know this. I stole $700 and unwrapped Christmas gifts from the old woman and her 18-year-old grandson next door. Days afterward, I heard the old lady screaming at her grandson, asking him why he did it.

Months afterward, the grandson caught my eye while I was spying on him from my bedroom window. He gave me a look from the sidewalk that said, *It was you, it was you who did that thievery, I know 'cause I can see it on your face.* Nothing ever came of it, though.

Years later, I learned he was stabbed to death during an attempted robbery in a park. Some time after that, the old lady died, too.

Michelle and I took a road trip up to Penn State, where her brother Brett was studying. By this time, she and I were into getting drunk and fucking. It was a mutually beneficial arrangement: She would get me drunk and I'd give her sex.

At one point during our visit, Brett left the dorm room, so naturally, Michelle and I drank beer and screwed … and we caught crabs from their toilet seat.

About a week or two later, back at the house in Mt. Washington, my roommates and I experimented with acid. This shit was wicked. It's a tiny piece of paper you place under your tongue. It takes 30 minutes to get started, then doesn't quit for six hours. You see waves upon waves in the room, and should you look at a picture of the ocean, it will start to move on its own.

Someone even brought over a Salvador Dali picture book to look at during this acid trip. His paintings are a trip all by themselves, let alone on acid!

During these six hours, we all ended up in my attic bedroom having a good time… until someone found my Quail lotion cure bottle for the crabs, which I had been hiding from my roommates. Crabs are the last thing you want to see or even talk about, whether you're on acid or not. How embarrassing that was! They all ran downstairs so fast. It was hard for me to rejoin that party downstairs.

No one wanted to sit next to me at first, but then we began to relax. Thank God, that trip finally ended. So embarrassing!

Michael

My roommate Steven helped me get my second job at Mrs. Field's Cookies at One Oxford Center, downtown. The building was 45 stories tall. I loved the smell of the place! I worked there for almost a year but I couldn't tolerate the racism I received from an angry black coworker.

She was trippin' hard again, like always, behind the manager's back, of course. She got mad at me for something, but what I do remember is her slamming my fingers in the swinging door to the entrance and calling me a honky. That was a first for me.

While working one morning at Mrs. Field's, I was taking my favorite cookies – the oatmeal-walnut-raisin ones – out of the oven when this man I knew walked by and stopped my world completely.

Let me back up a bit. When I was with my college rescuers a year before, they once drove me across town to the suburbs for a one-hour visit with Michael Clark – the guy who sent me that porno card in the mail while I was at that group home in Mars, Pennsylvania.

Michael's family had bought a house and he was eager to show off his new upstairs bedroom. We went into his bedroom and there was that iconic poster of Farrah Fawcett in her red bathing suit, right above his bed. *What the hell is that doing there? My Michael likes dick, not tits!* But I said nothing. I think I saw a football or a baseball bat in one of the corners of the room. Then it hit me. *Oh my God! My Michael's living a double life, and he's giving me front-row seats into his own life movie.*

We left that bedroom, whose was it? I don't know, certainly not the Michael I knew. We took off for the woods down the street and we blew each other.

He said my dick had gotten bigger. I thanked him. His seemed to be a little smaller, that's what the back of my throat said. Then out of the blue he admitted he'd been sad and had tried to kill himself twice.

I laughed at him to try to change his mood. It worked a little.

I said, "Cut that out. Don't think like that."

He changed the subject and a little while later he walked home. My friends were in the car waiting to pick me up.

Another time, Michael visited me downtown, for about five minutes. I was homeless at the time, but I didn't tell him. I couldn't. I kinda thought he knew, though. But he was a gentleman, and didn't say anything.

Now much later after that I was visiting a new friend, Larry Lumpkin, who lived near Pitt College and had been giving me free blow jobs for over a year.

Michelle came downstairs into Larry's apartment.

"My sister goes to school with a friend of yours, Michael Clark. You know him right?" she asked.

"Yeah, why? What's up?"

"He's dead, Darren. He killed himself. Turned the car on in the garage and didn't open the garage door."

Her words hit me like an army boot to the gut. I lost it. My beautiful red-headed curly-haired Michael – who wanted to be an architect, who wanted to change the world, who was damn good at gymnastics, who dreamed bigger than me – was gone! I ran upstairs, outside and sat on the stoop and cried right in front of the college students passing by. Just bawling. I couldn't move.

Michelle took me to Michael's funeral and stayed in her car. I walked in and didn't recognize a single face from Baldwin Whitehall Township, so I began relaxing, slowly making my way to the casket, believing it was some kind of terrible misunderstanding. *Michael's still alive and I'm about to look at some dead stranger, then get the hell out of there.*

The three people blocking my view parted ways and there he was, my Michael. My head dropped and the tears flew out of me. I ran for a chair near the exit and sat down and cried like the saddest little baby you ever did see, snots and all. All I wanted was to get as far away as I could from everyone in that room, especially that fucking body in that fucking box.

Fuck you, bigoted kids out there, I know you had a hand in this one, and I ain't gonna say shame on you. I say shame on your messed-up parents who teach you how to hate someone different than you. Fuck you!

Michael's mother brought a box of Kleenex over to me, and consoled me. I finally stopped crying and left that place. Michelle said I was in there for two hours. I swore I was there for only 10 minutes.

The man I recognized in front of Mrs. Fields Cookies was Michael's father. He looked kind of like Tom Selleck. We said hi to each other. I think he said he worked in the building, which thrilled me because now, at least to my reasoning, we could talk about our Michael every morning. That was what I so hoped for... but he never came by my cookie stand ever again. Sorry, Michael's Dad, I miss him too, every day. I Love you, Michael.

Rest in Peace, Michael J. Clark. I gotta set you free, my baby.

Florida, Here We Come!

When I turned 18, two things happened. One, I got my G.E.D. – by the skin of my teeth. Two, Michelle graduated college with a degree in education. Her parents barred me from her graduation ceremony, but I snuck in and watched from the balcony. I don't think I ever told her that.

Soon afterward, Michelle was hired by a school in Florida to teach kindergarten. She threatened to kill herself if I didn't go with her; plus, she pointed out, I'd probably turn into a drug addict if I stayed in Pittsburgh. So it was time to move to Fort Myers, Florida.

I said a tearful goodbye to my rescuers, Steven, Robin and Cindy. I will always Love them, for so many reasons. They taught me how to steal hearts better, live better and Love my gay self better. They also introduced me to new-wave music: The Cure, Dead Kennedys and my favorite, Kate Bush. Her song "Army Dreamers" is one of the best, most intense anti-war songs I've ever heard. Another song of hers that rocks is "Running Up That Hill."

Michelle and I left, not looking back, heading for the Sunshine State.

Now, the time in Florida would be a world I would have loved to destroy with invisible toys guns. I didn't want to be there. Not one day. But I stayed for close to 20 years. First thing I did was adopt Southern lingo, in order to hide my Pittsburgh past. I didn't do it because I was ashamed, or embarrassed. It was more like I never had a personal proud accomplishment to wear in my heart. I mean, come on, let's be honest: They don't hold G.E.D. graduation parties for orphan hooker boys. I know getting my G.E.D. was a good thing, but whenever I filled out an application to anywhere, I was always reminded by those questions that I didn't graduate from any school at all.

Michelle and I made the 1,143-mile trip with ease. We moved into a duplex on Mississippi Ave. with no one living next door. My first job was to find a drug dealer to get us some weed. My second job was to get a job to pay for the weed. That, too, was easy. Michelle was the bread-winner and I was the weed runner. I became a bag boy at the local grocery store. I held the job for a few days 'til a Spanish bag boy next to me called me a *maricón*, then left for the break room.

Deep down, I knew what the fuck he said; I just was looking for the right time to quit this job. I hated the restocking and the unloading of the trucks (which I was unaware was a requirement to begin with – they surprised me on that one, they did). The only good part about being a bag boy was the retrieving of the shopping carts. You could walk as slow as you wanted, and get in a smoke break. But back to the "*maricón*" comment.

I asked loudly to the patrons in line buying their groceries (who were all little Spanish women), "Who knows what *maricón* means? That kid who was just here called me that."

They all blushed and turned away.

Yup, I was on the right track. "*Maricón, maricón.* Who knows what that means, please?" I said, not lowering my volume.

Finally a younger woman I was bagging for leaned into my ear and whispered, "It means 'faggot.'"

Bingo! I knew it. I finished bagging her groceries and thanked her with a soft heart.

Then I went to the break room and found that boy who distributes trash talk and runs away like a bitch.

"Hey you," I said, interrupting his potato chip bite. "If you wanna call me a faggot, by all means, do so. But don't you *ever* do it in a language you think I don't understand. Unless you're really asking me if I wanna go outside and fight. Is that what you're asking me?"

All this time, I was screaming to myself, *Shut up! Are you stupid? You very well know this younger-than-you Spanish schoolboy has got to have at least six or seven brothers in the parking lot, waiting to pick him up tonight. Shut up, Darren!*

Just then, with one long breath, and a soft heart in return, he said, "I'm sorry."

It dawned on me he was having a bad day and no fight was going to fix that.

I shook his hand and said, "Ahh, don't worry about it. It's all good."

When I left the break room, I went straight to the manager's open-space office at the front of the store and told him what went down. And I quit. First job I ever walked out on.

An Open Letter to Pittsburgh

Dear Pittsburgh, Pennsylvania,

Thank you for giving me a beautiful place to grow up. I miss your four seasons, I miss your cool nights. I love how you intertwined the country with the city, the suburbs and the rivers that run through. I'm so proud of your beautiful leaves that grow on your trees every year. It reminds me of Christmas. Only you don't get one gift, you get thousands of green gifts. Please let me brag about your dirt. You allowed me to make the most beautiful mud pies ever. Haha, look at me now, I got tears filled up in my eyes 'cause I can see you all around me right this minute.

I'm up in Mt. Washington right this second at the Overlook. Staring out to that beautiful city that held me so close to Her Heart. I am still addicted to your glimmering city when the sun is high, you Sparkle like a Dancing Disco Ball. Now people, let me brag on my beautiful Pittsburgh Lovers. You Rock My World. I Love how you Love each other there, you're a winding smooth road, with splash-filled encouragements. I Love that you held my hand, and raised me up. Thank you, and I will always Love you.

Working Hard, Playing Harder (and Faking It) in Fort Myers

Early on in my time in Florida, I was friends with these two other derelicts, who turned me onto cough medicine thrills. We each stole a large bottle and drank it all down with a stolen gallon of milk as a chaser.

We got pulled over by the Fort Myers Beach police. They asked us to get out of the car and asked if we'd been drinking. No drinking, no smoking, no nothin'.

I blew in the officer's face to prove my innocence. Then I asked him if I could sit down because I was tired. I wasn't only tired, I was high as a kite. To my surprise he agreed. I began to crawl on top of the hood of the car, up over the windshield and sat on top of the car with my legs dangling over the side.

The officers couldn't figure out what to give us a ticket for, so they said, "I don't know what y'all have been up to, but get that kid on top of the car off these streets. He ain't playing with a full deck."

We laughed about that the whole ride home.

From when I was 18 until I turned 21, Michelle and I tried our hardest to fake it as a couple. I can only assume the relationship was convenient, for us both. I went back into the gay closet for three years. To be honest, however, Fort Myers, Florida, was (and still is, I think) a good ol' boys club kind of town. Being gay, loud and proud was not this town at all. But I do remember seeing rectangular rainbow-colored bumper stickers beginning to pop up. I knew what they were, and I was pissed I didn't have one of those gay advertising stickers on my car.

In those three years, one of my many jobs was working as a cook in a restaurant named Filthy Mc Nasty's, which later became a strip club. I was a Domino's pizza-delivery driver. I was also sent out to be a day laborer on construction sites three times, 'til a foreman liked my work abilities.

"Where you from?" he asked.

"Pittsburgh."

"You guys from Pittsburgh work like dogs," he said.

I barked at him and got the job as a mason tender, which means you mix cement for the block layers and set up their blocks for them to grab and set. If you made the mortar wrong, they'd dump it on the ground right in front of you and everyone, and make you mix up a new batch.

I liked that job a lot. You couldn't be dumb enough for this job, and they paid well, seven bucks an hour, not like that $2.50 hourly wage at the grocery store. It was fun, but it was hard work.

Around this same time, Pee-Wee Herman, my holy grail of a guy, was really popular. So of course I started to carry a bright red Pee-Wee Herman kids' lunch box to work every day with one of the five peanut butter and strawberry jelly sandwiches I prepared and froze every week without change for like two years.

From then on at work my new nickname was Pee-Wee. I Loved it like a superhero's cape.

I was 20 when I got my driver's license and my first new-to-me used car. It was a lemon of a car for three hundred bucks. It died in the driveway the second we got it home. The following day we returned the car for a re-fund, which was quickly denied. A week later, around 9 p.m., I went back with a friend to that used-car dealership and flattened all of his cars' tires.

When I was starting to break up with Michelle, I suggested she date a guy who was, at that time, my best friend. He'd recently dumped his girlfriend… put her on a bus and told her to scram.

He and Michelle got together while I took a long trip to Pittsburgh, but I didn't learn of that for awhile. You see, during those three years Michelle would occasionally travel home back to Pittsburgh because she could afford it. Or her folks would send her, and only her, a plane ticket to come home and visit. So I was really homesick, but before I made it to Pittsburgh I got even sicker, physically, on the Greyhound bus I rode. I wanted to try to sleep the whole way because I hated that bus. So I took seven sleeping pills to really knock me out. I awoke about three hours later, in the back of the bus, on the floor, having convulsions that lasted about an hour. I was sure I was a goner. What the hell was I thinking?

After that damn sleepless bus ride, I had planned to be in Pittsburgh for about 30 days, so I needed a job to support myself. I somehow got hooked up at a doughnut factory. This was awesome. I got one of my many dream jobs I always secretly wanted, but never told anyone.

I was in charge of filling cherry-filled doughnuts. That's my favorite doughnut and it was one of my favorite jobs, too – until the young teenage punk floor manager made fun of me in front of everyone in the locker room. He told everyone I was talking to myself while working.

I'll admit I was. I'm a thinker and sometimes when you talk to God, and think to yourself, your lips move. So what? Again I was looking for a way out of this job and wanted to go back to Michelle and try to make things work with us. So I set up a meeting with the that floor manager and his boss, up in the second-floor office that overlooked the factory.

I asked the big boss, "Could I be frank and speak from the heart?"

"Yes," he said. "I wish you would."

I turned to the kid and said, "What the fuck is wrong with you? Aren't we supposed to be a team up in here? I wanted to be your friend, I really liked you." Then I turned to the big boss and said, "If you guys keep hiring motherfuckers like him, your factory will die."

Then I quit and walked out. And for the record, I was right: That doughnut factory shut down less than a year later.

When my Greyhound bus pulled into the terminal in Fort Myers, Michelle was there to pick me up. The whole time I'd been in Pittsburgh, whenever we talked on the phone, I could tell she was trying to find the words to break up with me, without saying those actual words. But she said them immediately after we kissed hello in the car. It was over. I could feel it through her lips.

We drove back to our duplex and she professed her love for my best friend while he listened in on us from outside the window, crouched under a bush. I want to call him a coward for being like that, but really I'll give it to God. If I had known what was really going on while I was up in Pittsburgh, I would never have come back to Florida.

Finding God... and Hypocrisy in Bible School

Once I was finally on my own in Fort Meyers, I turned to religion as a source of comfort. I attended a church down the street, next to a Dairy Queen. The church claimed they were non-denominational but anyone could clearly see they were Pentecostal. They were all white people, but rocked like a black church, it was amazing. Except when the pastor tried to sell me Amway. That part sucked.

During my time at that church, I sang in the choir for one summer. But one bomb of a performance in front of the congregation was my last one and I wouldn't sing in front of anyone again 'til I was in my 30s.

At that church, a fellow member approached me and asked if I'd like to attend a Bible college in the middle of the state, in Groveland, Florida.

I told him I couldn't afford it.

"No problem," he said. "The school helps students with their tuition."

Now back when I was living at Mars Presbyterian Home for Children, up in that mansion, that counselor named Bill (who had nicknamed me Brain Tumor Numer), told all of us kids, "If you ever get the opportunity to go to college, don't ever let it pass you by. Jump on it."

So I did. Plus I was tired of chasing this beautiful girl named Jenny. My eyes and my heart Loved her, but my dick didn't.

The night before I left for Bible college, I got good and drunk. I didn't think they would be serving alcohol at this non-denominational Bible college (they were basically Pentecostal too). Ladies were required to wear dresses and the men wore dress pants all the time. They were a little weird like that.

But hell, they were giving me tuition, food, room and board, so I didn't say anything.

The following morning, the guy who got me this college gig and his son drove me to the school in their shiny maroon pimped-out truck with all my belongings loaded in the flat bed. I left my one-room apartment in shambles (sorry, landlord). Because I was hung over, too, they stuck me in the bed of the truck, where I slept during the whole four-hour drive. I guess my beer breath might have had something to do with it, too. And they bought me breakfast and coffee before we rolled onto campus, to sober me up. They were so pissed! I could see it on their faces as they dropped me off.

School had already been in session for about six weeks. This sucked because once again in my life, I was behind. And I never managed to catch up. I failed every class except Proper Etiquette and Public Speaking Class.

I do have a few good memories of this school. One is a family named Thomas. They were a family of five from West Virginia. The parents were both attending the school and their whole family (their kids were all girls) was provided a small cement-block cottage to live in. They would diligently assist me in my studies. They also let me call them Mom and Dad. I Love and miss them.

Another memory is of the Millers; they were a newlywed couple with a newborn. They had their own cottage too. Brother Miller, maybe 23 years old, nicknamed me Scooter. When he'd walk by my dorm-room window, almost every day, he would yell out, "Scooooooter." I miss him, too. He was this big linebacker of a white guy with soft, short Army-cut red hair. He loved picking me up and spinning me. I loved it too.

At the end of that school term, I quit right before

final exams. I knew I was failing, so why would I take a test to prove that? I asked Brother Miller to drive me to the bus station. I told him there was an emergency in Fort Myers I had to attend to.

He did, even though I'm pretty sure he knew I was lying.

I seldom masturbated at that school 'til the end. One Saturday night I finally jerked off, and then felt so guilty about it. Then the next morning in church, the preacher's wife – a tiny little 80-year-old white woman who was vice president of the school – stood at the podium and said, "There's an evil spirit lurking around the campus."

Now I'd been an emotional wreck at this school all year long because of my past and dealing with the blessings of being at a college to begin with. I'd cry at the drop of a hat, so of course I swore the evil spirit was me!

The vice president asked, "Does someone have something to confess? We're not continuing any further 'til someone speaks up."

So of course I started to cry. I was almost ready to stand and confess my hairy palms, when all of a sudden, a fellow dorm mate stood up, bawling, and blurted out, "I masturbated last night and I'm sorry."

I almost fell out of my chair. I quickly hid my tears and started laughing in my head. This was too much to handle.

There was a giant lake next to the school, with a canoe. I once took the canoe around to a section where no one could see me and I jerked off. To my surprise, when I looked over the edge of the boat, I saw 10 alligators watching me. That scared the piss out of me! I intended never to go back there again... well maybe just once more.

There were only two black people at our college: a tall female student and a tall heavyset young teacher who used to be a student there. He once told me he wasn't gay, when I admitted I was. I didn't believe him because he was queenier than that famous drag-queen, RuPaul. I actually confessed that to the president when I first arrived. We all had to give up our secrets to him before joining that school. The pastor said he wouldn't tell anyone, but he lied to me; they all knew.

The school set up those two to go steady. I later heard they got married... but they divorced a year later. Who would have expected that, huh?

At the very end of my time at bible school, there was this young woman named Kathy. I Loved her, even though no one else did. She was definitely different from all the rest. She was a short white girl with brown, nappy hair. She wore thick, pointy, '50s-style old-lady glasses and had a chronic sniffling problem. She also had the highest, squeakiest little mouse voice you ever did hear, but I loved it. Mind you, there were maybe only 20 students at this college. Half boys, half girls. Most of the girls were stuck-up pretty little bitches who would laugh and make fun of my Kathy.

This one time, crying on a bench, Kathy told me she knew she was the outcast in her dorm, and the other girls ignored her and wouldn't include her in any of the reindeer games.

One night, after hearing a ton of giggling from the girls' dorm next door, I got up, went over there and knocked on the door.

When they opened the door, sure enough, there was my Kathy, lying in her bunk, while all the other girls huddled together on the other side of the room. I asked them if I could speak to all of them, they said yes.

I asked, "Why are you always treating your sister Kathy so poorly?"

This must have been a little embarrassing for Kathy, but she didn't stop me.

The other girls tried to deny it.

I said, "Well then, why is Kathy crying to me as to how mean you guys are to her, and you know you are. You don't even sit next to her at lunch, dinner or church. Am I lying?"

Then they all gathered around my Kathy and half-heartedly apologized.

I think I saw my Kathy cry for joy a little.

I winked at her and left, but not before I told them all, "Kathy's got more God in her little pinky than all of you put together; so whenever you mess with her, you're messing with God."

I Love and miss you, Kathy. I miss your hugs.

Kathy was also the last to see me leave the campus for good. Two weeks after school let out for the summer, I drove back there early, early in the morning, to retrieve the belongings I had left behind. A few students were there for the summer, but they were all asleep. Interesting, I could feel the spirit of sleep all upon the dorm, and knew no one was going to wake up as I moved out, really. I felt it to be my Daniel in the Lion's den moment Bizarre, huh?

I snuck into my old dorm room and got everything out. On my last trip to my car, there, sitting on the bench between our dorms, was my Kathy.

"Hey girl, what'cha doing there all alone?" I said, catching her by surprise.

We hugged and cried, then talked for like 15 minutes. She asked me not to quit school.

I said, "I won't. If the school asks me to come back, I will."

You know that never happened.

Listening to the Voice of God

So after I quit Bible college, guess who took me into their home so I wouldn't be homeless?

Michelle and my former best friend.

My 21st birthday was at the end of August and I was still attending that non-denominational church. The church people asked if I'd be an adult church counselor on a field trip to Tampa.

I remember feeling pissed because I wanted to be on the kids' side of this trip. But I wasn't a kid anymore, I was turning 21 and needed to grow up.

We were going on the streets to testify for Jesus and save souls. We gathered at 4 a.m. in two rented vans, five adults and 10 kids. The trip took a few hours and when we made it to the church in Tampa, our host took us to their campsite near the church. Girls in one cottage, the boys and me in another.

After dinner we had a short rest and then we got dressed up for Wednesday-night church services.

In church, it's a big kind of round space, the seats were 20 percent full, and the kids and I were sitting in the middle of the church behind everyone else. So guess who shows up in my mind... the Universe. This had happened to me a few times before in church, like the voice would tell me to go over to a stranger with the red shoes on and just hold her hand, something like that. So I did and the moment our hands touched, she broke down and cried all over me.

So now in this church, the voice asked if I Love him.

I said earlier, I adopted God as my Father on that cold, wet, muddy hill in Pittsburgh as a child. I've always talked to the voice as if it were my best friend.

So I talked back to Dad and said, "Oh my god, what are you doing here? Don't bother me, I'm trying to worship you."

He said, "I said, do you Love me?"

I replied, "You know I Love you. What do you want?"

"I want you to lie down in the middle of the aisle for me."

"You gotta be joking, Pops, I ain't doing that," I said back.

"Oh, so you don't Love me?"

"I didn't say that," I replied.

"What do you have to lose? Your pride? Come on, no one's looking, just your kids behind you, but they don't care."

So I did. I arose slowly and stood in the middle of the aisle, turned toward the exit sign, knelt down, lay on my belly, closed my eyes and touched my nose to the floor.

Instantaneously I was transported out of my body and through a dark tunnel. I began to cry uncontrollably while flying through that tunnel. The closest I can compare this experience to is the 1997 movie, *Contact*, starring Jodie Foster. There's a scene where Jodie's character falls through what I think is a wormhole. That was the same feeling I was experiencing – except, I didn't see any colors. Everything was dark. That's why I cried. Another way of explaining it is comparing it to an infant who gets startled upon being picked up from the ground and begins to cry.

After two minutes, the voice hushed to me softly, as if to an infant, reassuring me all was okay. "Relax I got you," it said to me.

The voice asked if he could put me through the

wringer one last time, and also said, "Will you let me put you on drugs? You're gonna steal and get caught, and I will turn all your friends against you."

I finally stopped crying and accepted I was floating in the air somewhere.

I said back to the entity, "I don't know about that."

"Fine, fine," he replied. "I'll see if some else wants the part."

"No wait," I said back. "When you say drugs, what kind are you talking about?"

The voice said, "The kind your brother Ricky's on, only I'm gonna put you on it for close to 20 years. After that time is over, I will remove it from you, and when it's all over, will you please remember me?"

I said, "Oh my God, you gotta be kidding me! I... I... I... okay, I'll do it."

I agreed to this because of one thing. I knew this was real, I can't lie. It was an honor to be chosen. I knew that. I don't know why the Universe chose me, but I felt LOVE through my whole body. I had no fear of what took over me but was well knowing it would never harm me or anyone.

I felt Jesus, Buddha, God, was not its true name. He and She are named Love. I wasn't scared at all.

I began to blink and open my eyes, I was back in the middle of the aisle in that church.

I got up off the floor facing that exit sign in relief and disbelief. I slowly turned my head, I looked at the whole congregation and thought, *They won't believe what just happened to me, none of them. God,* I thought, *they really have no idea how important they are to each other. Not a fucking clue, and they're so scared to Love each other.*

Allow me to press upon your hearts – to all of you. Love each other, Love each other, Love each other hard. Don't just get along. *Love each other,* my beautiful brothers and sisters. Know how special you are, from head to toe.

I walked out of the church as they were passing the

collection plate. I pushed through the double wooden doors. They closed behind me and I paced back and forth in the foyer, alone.

I called out to Dad. "God?"

"Yes?"

"Did that just really happen?"

"You know it did," he replied.

"Can you take me on that ride again?"

"Yes," he said, to my surprise.

I got down on the ground, lay on my belly again, closed my eyes, touched my nose to the ground and swissshhh – off into that tunnel I went again.

It was scary at first, but I didn't cry this time. I got up and down a few more times but the vision was fading, and the church service was ending.

When my pastor's daughter came into the foyer, I grabbed her hand. "Can I tell you something that just happened?" We walked outside through the grass. I told her I'd just had a vision quest experience.

She looked at me with no words.

I tried to tell her about it but I had this feeling she wasn't hearing me.

I was right. A year later I reminded her about that time; she said she had no memory of it.

My Last Act of Animal Abuse

I have this theory that we all have what I call a "sensitivity button." Well, mine was seriously out of whack! But I credit God – the Great Doctor, the King of the operating room – and Randy for the major healing in my life.

I used to beat the fuck out of my dogs when no one was looking. I had this temper that was not fair to unleash against an animal, but I did it anyway. Beneath my cheerful exterior was all the shit I carried around from my past. And I took it out on my helpless animals. I became the ultimate bully.

One afternoon in the mid 1990s, I was weed whacking next to the fence out back and our new dog was barking at the high-speed spinning plastic threads.

I hollered at her, "Don't! Get away!"

Three times she ignored me, and I was getting tired of yelling, so I figured I'd teach her a lesson.

When she turned around, I zapped her butt.

What the fuck was I thinking?

I shut the weed whacker off and tended to the five angry red stripes on my little dog's ass.

I never abused a dog after that, and it's been over 20 years.

Now what would make a coward like me do shit like that? I think I probably just answered that: I was a coward. I loved wrong and not right. I tell everyone I can't stand physical violence, but behind closed doors I didn't practice what I preached.

What's the cure?

I can't speak for others. But I say this because it's what worked for me: Tattle on yourself. This is the cure. Tattle, tattle, tattle on yourself. Tell your shit to a therapist. Your preacher. Your parent. Your best friend. It works. It's scary-ass shit, but it has to be done. And it works. It worked for me.

I told Randy what I did.

"Are you gonna do it again?" he asked.

I said no, and that's when my healing began.

We all do wrong stuff – in one form or another. Unless maybe you're one of the lucky ones, and you aren't troubled, then believe me, God bless you. Sounds like you were Loved good.

My New Best Friend, Bo

I was fresh out of Bible college, I managed to block out that crazy vision and my new four-footed best friend had just shown up: Bo, a beautiful homeless Rottweiler-mix dog. Are you ready for this? I prayed for this dog just the day before. I was lonely and I just wanted a special friend. I found him outside next to the apartment's dumpster. Just unbelievable.

Michelle, her boyfriend and I placed an ad in the lost and found to see if anyone was missing him. No one answered – thank you, God.

He was mine, all mine!

At first I called him Mercedes, but that didn't seem to fit him. Then I called him Bo, and he responded to that name right away, so Bo it was. We were inseparable, he went everywhere I went, and a friend from church had just given me a big old green, two-door '70s Cadillac. So you know Bo and I were styling in Fort Myers!

I still didn't have a job, but I had to buy gas and pay my share of the rent. I got this crazy notion that if I went from home to home, I could maybe collect donations for my college tuition. Heck, I was no stranger to begging for money. It would be easy.

Wrong!

At the first six homes, everyone turned me down, with sick looks on their faces, like, *You weird little man! Get away.*

At the seventh house I met this little old lady

named Annie, who could have been Granny's twin from *The Beverly Hillbillies*.

When I asked her for a donation, she replied, "Do you do windows?"

Quick as fly I said, "Yes. Yes I do."

She invited me in and fed me milk and cookies – no lie! She *actually* gave me milk and cookies. I don't know who was more in need of whom.

At this point, I was starting to creep back out of the gay closet. When that happened, my "friends" in church began to turn on me.

They were mostly young, but effective with hurling insults. One of them left this message on my answering machine: "Hey faggot, why don't you go back to Pittsburgh and go get butt fucked?"

To escape their hurtful comments, I spent a lot of my time with Annie – at Taco Bell, at the movies or just walking with her and her Jack Russell terrier. Annie was always walking that old fellow. But on a sad note, she and her dog would be killed by a hit-and-run driver while they were crossing the road. May you both rest in peace.

I finally got a job with T&S Construction. They were my lifesavers! They hired and fired me three times in a two-year period.

I was young and really emotional and having bad days with fools I surrounded myself with. So I took it out on my job. I didn't care that they fired me; I was amazed that they would rehire me. I compared that experience to a baseball game. I didn't care that I struck out three times; I was honored to have been a part of their team. That job allowed me to rent my own little house, for Bo and me. We held onto that home as long as we could, but I was still a juvenile asshole at heart.

When you're in your 20s and acting like a cocky, arrogant thief, you eventually pay the price, one way or another. I got caught stealing a watch from the mall and spent a weekend in jail.

Going to jail seemed to be a habit for me. Getting caught for this or that, driving without insurance would have its way with me; and then when you don't pay the fines for your crimes, you end up doing the time... I ended up doing a few 30-day stints in the county lockup.

That really sucked, but with a twist.

I read a book in there, it was called *The Firm*. It was awesome, I'd really never read a book from cover to cover before, and I felt proud of myself. When visitation day came on Sundays, guess who visited? Annie, God Love her. Michelle and her boyfriend visited, too, but I think he enjoyed seeing me behind bars, in a small, sick way. I could feel it.

They got married, but I didn't believe the marriage would last, so when they invited me, I didn't go. Turns out I was right. He left her for a stripper (years later he bragged to me he banged her on stage in front of the whole strip club) soon after, and with $2,000 in debt to the company he stole from while working for them. Get this: Michelle paid it off for him.

Now when I was home, Bo was home; but if I had to go somewhere, he would escape and come find me, every time. I was once seven blocks away in the Route 80 Diner off Palm Beach Boulevard. And through the back door, who comes strolling in? Bo.

Sometimes he didn't find me, and I'd have to go looking for him. One time, I was headed to jail and Bo had been on the milk carton again. Before I got out, my friend Cathy heard him howling in someone's backyard, like he always did whenever a fire truck passed by with its siren blaring. When I got out of jail, Cathy put a big red bow around Bo's neck and surprised me with him.

Two Major Life Changes...
One Horrible, One Good

Within a one-week time period, I would meet two people. One was Tomas; the other was Randy.

I met Tomas at a gay bar. We didn't have sex right away, but he seemed nuts for me. I was into him, too. The night we met, we talked 'til 4 in the morning. We really got along great, but he lived with his mom, who didn't like me big-time. I could tell, because she always had a scowl on her face whenever I was around. Tomas had a boyfriend himself, so why he wanted me at all confused the hell out of me.

Then there was Randy.

My friend Mice and I had been walking Bo. We were about to leave the park in the back of Pine Manor, heading home, when I spotted this handsome guy in green shorts, a white Ocean Pacific tank top and no shoes, sitting on the edge of a boat, playing fetch with his black Labrador retriever.

I'd been talking to God for the past year, asking him for a life partner. Every time I met someone I liked, I would ask God if he was mine. I really would.

And every time, I'd hear a big fat "No."

Scared I was going to hear another no, I didn't ask... yet.

I tried flirting a little. No luck. The guy was more interested in playing fetch with his dog.

Randy would say, "Watch this." He would throw a tennis ball into a 10-foot-high brush patch and Bart (his dog) would jump in after it. He'd return with the ball every time.

Then Randy gave me the ball to throw for Bart; yup, he returned like a pro.

After a while, Mice and I started to head back home, because I had to go to work.

Randy said, "If ya wanna come over some time, even tonight, just knock on my door."

"Okay," I said. "Maybe."

As Mice and I headed home, he was walking Bo so I fell back a little and asked God if Randy was the one for me.

Before I could finish the question, he said, "Yes,"

That shocked me. You see, Randy looked like a college preppie living on the poor side of Fort Myers – like drug dealer-side poor. But who cares? Dad said *Yes!*.

I started to spin around in the tall grass… but then came more to the story.

God said, "All I ask of you is that you don't tell anyone for two years. Not one person."

I didn't.

But I did crawl through Randy's back window that very night. I had to.

When I got there, he told me, "I can't have my neighbors seeing you come in my front door."

Wow, I didn't see that coming, but I did as he asked. I crawled through that window for weeks.

Eventually, he introduced me to the neighbors and allowed me to use the front door. But according to Randy, I was "just a friend." This pissed me off, but I also kind of understood. Anyhow, he was mine and that was that.

Randy was a great guy and everyone liked him… except Tomas. He hated him – with a vengeance! Jealousy was the leader.

At the time, Bo and I were living with a guy who had his own double-wide trailer. One morning, after a night of drinking with friends, I woke up to find every stitch of clothing in my closet gone, hangers and all. Worse than that, Bo was missing.

Tomas had stolen all my clothes, and managed to take Bo without me waking up. The guy liked his whiskey, and it showed that night. He threw all my clothes out on the side of the highway as he drove two hours out of town. He dumped Bo out near an old rodeo stadium.

After calling him for three days, I finally went to his mom's place because whenever I called, his mom kept saying he wasn't home.

He was.

Tomas came out to the driveway and told me what he had done. Ready for this? Meanwhile, his mom stood in front of the living-room window, holding a shotgun.

I told Tomas, "You know Bo's dead."

He said, "No he's not, I just kicked him out of the car."

I shook my head. "Nope. I can feel it. He's gone."

The next morning, I went to the town where he said he'd left him. I looked for the animal rescue shelter to see if they had any information on my Bo. It was a small town with a puny animal shelter.

I went in with a picture of Bo and asked, "Have ya'll seen this dog?"

They said no.

I got into my car to leave and the small voice came to me. "Go back in there and ask them one more time."

I did.

They asked me to sit down and said, "A guy was just in here." They described him; it was Tomas.

He told them I was on my way and asked that they please not tell me they'd put Bo to sleep.

They'd picked up a Rottweiler mix from the local rodeo four days earlier.

"Somehow he had snuck into the arena while the show was going on," they admitted. "He went into the middle of the ring and started howling, so they called us up and we brought him in."

They said he never stopped howling.

"Sir," they told me, "our policy here at the animal shelter is, because it's a small town, if no one comes to pick the dog up after three days, we have to put them down; we don't have enough room for all the animals. We're very sorry."

I didn't believe them. I held back my tears until I got into the car, then I bawled all the way home... but not before forgiving Tomas almost immediately. I did that for two reasons. One, I didn't want to act out of malicious revenge on another human and end up in jail. It wouldn't have brought Bo back to life. Two, my heart really went out to the pain of anyone who carries the burden of those types of memories.

I called up my boss at A Taste of New York Pizza, where I was a pizza-delivery guy. I said "I'm at the bar. I'm getting drunk; my dog was just killed."

They said to me, "If you don't come in, you're fired."

I was fired.

Rest in peace my soft teddy bear, Bo. I Love you.

Seeing Things?

This is a story I rarely share – about the time I saw UFOs. I almost couldn't believe it, but I wasn't alone when I saw them. It happened a month before I met Randy. I was dating this big tall Irish redhead police officer named Patrick. He loved picking me up in his green T-top Camaro and taking me out to eat. He also loved to speed down the road; he said most cops speed.

This one time we were headed across the South Cleveland Ave. Bridge, on US-41, heading toward N. Fort Myers. We pulled over at the corner of N. Key Drive and US-41, looking west, around 7 p.m. We watched what appeared to be two flying saucers floating in the sky. I couldn't believe it, either, but they were there. Patrick saw them first. We got out of the car and pointed them out to people passing by at the stop sign. There were two of them and they looked to be about a mile away, way up in the air. They were shaped like saucers, with multi colors swirling. They turned to green, yellow, blue, then red, continuously. They were mesmerizing, and they moved like flying mosquitoes, with amazing speed. It didn't look like anything man here on earth could make... yet. Who knows? We couldn't take our eyes off them, and we didn't want to, either.

After about 12 minutes, they flew off into space.

If that was a hoax, bravo, you got us good. If it was the real deal, then yup, we're definitely not alone.

So there's two stories before I go straight for the toilet paper-roll pipe for the first time. I'd made a new friend in Fort Myers, Brian Roamer. We met in a gay bar one afternoon after work, waiting on tables. He was about 5' 6" with a slender face and skinny body. He was a little bit queeny, but like a butch queen, if there's such a thing. Also, he wasn't ashamed to tell you he got AIDS. After some of the sexual escapades he told me about, I see how. Then again, I remember him telling me the dude who gave it to him didn't tell him. That happened a lot back then.

Well, this one afternoon, Brian and I were buzzing by 3 p.m. sitting at the bar. We'd been friends for a week or two. I don't know how we got on the subject about crack cocaine, but we did. I think we were talking about how someone was on it and we didn't care for them. So we started to sing a mean jingle about being a crackhead. We sang, "He's a crackhead, he's a crackhead," and so on. We sang this to the whole bar. Come to think of it, I think we were the only two people in there, aside from the bartender. Before we stopped singing, I remembered the vision I had back in that church, and the drug it was talking about, my brother's drug.

My brother Ricky had moved to Fort Myers a few years earlier. I knew he was smoking crack, because he'd have me drive him to pick up his crack, then he'd sit in the back seat and smoke it while I drove him to his apartment.

He told me, "Darren, don't you ever do this drug — you swear to me."

I didn't. I couldn't.

So after remembering that vision in the bar, I stopped singing with Brian. I also remember getting a *watch what you're saying* look from the bartender. I could feel it. I was seriously against crack, but we were all starting to snort coke. So obviously a gateway was being built.

I'll mention here that my friend Brian died from AIDS years later, all by himself in his bedroom, face down on the floor. Dear Bri-Bri, Rest in peace.

I'm gonna throw Randy under the bus here, with his permission of course. He was probably about the poorest guy I ever dated. He was busy paying off his parents ten grand for bailing him out of doing any prison time, after being busted for possession of cocaine.

Randy is the richest person I know. Even without a dime in his pocket, he can out-dollar-bill every one of us on any given day. Those who are his family and his friend, you already know this. Those who are his family and *not* his friend, that's sad. On both sides, I guarantee it. I've watched the tears fall down his face for the want of your compassion and Love. I do, too, but I'm not about to tell you. Nope, never, never, never. Well, maybe one day.

This particular time, Randy and I were on the outs. It was night time, Bo had just died. I was at the bar, listening to the jukebox. I had befriended two guys who were partners, also they had two pitchers of beer on their table. "Sit down," they said to me. I remember them telling me they sold pianos. They also asked me if I wanted to fool around and do some coke.

"Hell, yes," I said, and away we went to my place.

In my bedroom, one of the guys pulled out a tiny little zip-lock baggie. Right away I could see it wasn't looking right. Coke is white powder, but this shit was small light-yellow rock-looking things. Crack.

I looked at those two guys, shook my head and said, "No, I ain't doing that."

"Come on, you've never done this before? Sure you have."

I said, "No. y'all said coke; that ain't coke. Why did you lie to me?"

"Look, we can smash it up and it'll be like coke." So they did. Then they said, "But you gotta smoke it for it to work."

They made a homemade pipe from a toilet-paper roll and tin foil and a gum band (that's a rubber band for those of you who aren't from Pittsburgh). They wouldn't smoke any 'til I took the first hit. So I did. The feeling was unreal!

The high was intense and short, 30 seconds, maybe a minute. I never saw anyone else do what I did. I puked. I would vomit – in the toilet, in the trash can, in the sink – almost every time I took a hit of crack. After the drug was gone, so were they. Though the addiction was here to stay.

Texas

Randy's from Texas. And yes everything is bigger in Texas, especially emotions. The first time I went to Texas, to meet my in-laws, in the late 1990s. I went to the local library in Fort Myers, before our trip. I took out the novel *War and Peace*, to try to pretend I was an educated person, which if you know me, I'm not.

A few years later, we were on our third visit to Texas and it was the last time I was going to stand in front of them pretending to be something I wasn't, pretending not to be a couple. I wasn't ashamed of being gay, Randy on the other hand, well I wouldn't use the word *ashamed*. I would say he's not exactly comfortable making his parents completely uncomfortable.

And that's what I did when I professed my Love for him, when his dad asked me what I wanted from his son.

I said, "Love. The same kind of Love you have for your wife, that's the love I have for him."

The temperature in the room rose. Words came out of his mouth I didn't realize he knew.

I should have just said I just want a Mercedes Benz from him; they would have believed that more.

Then in a flash we were kicked to the curb.

Randy's cousin and his wife and kids let us sleep on their wooden floors that night, with soft, loving pillows. Thank you, guys.

That following morning we left early. The tears

flowed from both our eyes down our faces. While I was stopped at a light, a car pulled up next to us, with a fun-loving, laughing young guy. He was a skinny guy, maybe in his 20s, with long dirty-blond hair and sky-blue eyes. He looked like he might have just puffed on a joint. Anyhow, our eyes locked. His jolly demeanor left his face the second he saw me in pain. Our windows were down.

He said to me, "Hey, buddy, it's gonna be okay. Trust me, brother, it's gonna be okay." The light turned green, and off he went.

I'll never forget that guy's face and the compassion he bestowed upon me at that moment. Some stranger in Texas who didn't know me cared enough to say something. So to my brother out there in Texas, thank you from the bottom of my heart. You were right, everything did turn out okay.

An End to the Kleptomania

I had been so many times in county jail I knew the back seat of a squad car like an evangelist knows his own sin. The last time I was in jail was because of something stupid. It was mostly due to failure to pay driving fines, or driving without insurance too many times.

Randy and I were just passed up by Hurricane Charlie. It caused damage countywide, but north of us, Port Charlotte got it worst. A local grocery store was out for the count in business. A month or less after the storm, the grocery store had a huge sale, like 90 percent off everything, with a one-day announcement. So Randy and I flew down there and split up. He filled two bags. I headed for the health and beauty-aids aisle to fetch makeup and hair products. I'd recently been introduced to the drag-show stage and had become a bona fide stage performer. I didn't do drag, but I sang songs while performing silly skits.

My first night, one of the drag performers, Miss Whitney, had told me, "If you really want to perform on my stage, it will be tonight or never."

Thank you, Miss Whitney, for that motivational moment. Best ever.

That night I sang "The Rose" by Bette Midler, while pretending I was in my dressing room, shaving and preparing to go on stage. We hung an open frame from the ceiling with paper clips and fishing string to act as a mirror, and ended the show with a pretty plastic rose in my lapel that lit up.

So there I was, in line in this extremely crowded store. Randy was nowhere to be seen. That was when I realized I didn't have any money. I figured, "Huh, I'll just steal it."

I had already been in jail in different Florida cities for theft. Fort Myers, stealing a watch and Naples, stealing a T-shirt. God, was I stupid. After being in jail that last time I had a personal talk with the Big Guy upstairs. What I did was cry and beg for this thievery disease to leave me. I would literally get the shakes when I was in a store; just wanting to steal a pack of gum would physically give me the shakes. Something was way wrong.

So I was about to walk out of this store with these two bags – with the whole store looking like a tornado of people. It was a cake walk, just walk out that door.

Then a thought came to me. "You're gonna get busted."

So I stopped and stood there, between the cash register and the exit sign.

The store was loud but in my head, everything was silent.

I looked all around me. Another thought came to me. I felt like Randy was watching me but I couldn't see him. I thought, *If I put these bags down, I'll bet Randy shows up out of the blue.* I turned around and looked for an empty shelf. I set the bags down and headed for the door.

Outside the door, yup, was Randy.

Happy as a turtle driving a Ferrari, holding up his two bags, he said to me, "Look what I got." Then, seeing I wasn't holding any bags, he asked, "What did you get?"

"They didn't have anything I wanted," I replied with a shrug.

At that moment, my kleptomania measles were gone for good.

Pops and the Lighting Guy

One of my last times in jail in Florida, I was doing weekends – that means you show up to the county jail on Friday at 5 p.m., and turn yourself over to the authorities; then on Sunday night you go home, to return the following Friday.

I got permission to bring Charms Blow Pops for the inmates. Smoking was banned by then. I'd fan the Blow Pops out and tell my fellow jailbirds to pick whatever color they wanted.

The reds always went first... and fast. That's how I never got messed with. Lucky me.

In all my jail time, two incidents in particular stand out.

This one guy, who was in jail full time, asked me why I passed out the candy.

I said, "It's what I would want if I was doing full time in jail."

He smiled at me. "I used to work as a lighting guy" – or was he the sound guy? I don't remember, but it was something way up high he talked about. He told me he worked on *The Cosby Show*. Then he said, "There's this thing that actors have and you have it; You need to be on stage. Trust me. You need to go to Hollywood."

I just smiled as big as I could, and didn't say a word. That's what I remember of that guy.

Now this other guy, he let me call him Pops. He was an older man, maybe 60; tall and thin with medium-length grey hair. I'd say he looked like Jed Clampett on *The*

Beverly Hillbillies, but skinnier. He was finishing up 11 years in prison. He'd been transferred to the county jail to finish up his last few weeks.

One afternoon, I asked him, "Hey, Pops, what did you do eleven years for?"

We were sitting on his bed. He looked into my eyes and said, "Murder."

For some reason, I wasn't scared by this at all. If anything, again in life, (like back when Bo died) my heart grew closer to the pain that must come with that type of situation. So I asked him, "Was it the first time?"

He giggled and said, "Nope. I've killed seven times; some the cops know about, some they don't."

"Well, why did you do it?"

Without hesitation, he said, "They pissed me off."

We both began to laugh. He laughed from the heart; I laughed out of fear – and doing my absolute best to not piss him off.

Then he asked me, "Do you know where Mexico is?"

"Sure I do."

"I'm going there when I get out," he said. "I got three thousand dollars saved up, and when I get out, I'm headed there. I'm getting the hell out of the United States."

I asked, "Who's picking you up when you get out?"

"No one. I don't have any family left."

Why I said what I said next, I'll never know, but out of my mouth came, "Can I pick you up when you get released?"

He asked, "Are you sure, kid? You don't have to."

"I know, but I want to. You've been so kind to me, Pops."

I didn't tell him this, but if I were in his shoes, I'd be tickled pink if a little punk wanted to be my friend.

Two weeks later, at 5 a.m., in the dark, under the

144

streetlights downtown behind the Fort Myers County Jail, I waited in my car while the jail door opened to a small gathering of people greeting their little jailbirds' release.

Out came Pops, smiling from ear to ear, breathing in the free fresh air. I opened up the passenger-side door after we hugged. He hopped in.

"Where to?" I asked.

"To the bus station please," he said.

"Okay, but I have a treat for you first. I wanna take you to my special place; it's where I watch the sun come up. May I take you there, Pops?"

"Brother, take me anywhere, but let's get the hell out of here!"

Off we went, making our way down Highway 80 toward Tice Fort Myers, we then turned left onto Royal Palm Park Road. We drove as far as you can go 'til we got to a mini dock and pier. At dawn it is the best place to be in all of Fort Myers, overlooking the Caloosahatchee River and across from Beautiful Island. I walked Pops to the pier.

I said, "Enjoy, Pops. This is long overdue and it's all for you."

I heard him sniffle deep.

We stayed for 20 minutes, watching the clouds change colors from snowy white to warm orange and soft yellow pillows in the skies as the sun began to show off and move the atmosphere. The morning birds were flying by, ready to feast on the day. Steam rose from the almost-still waters.

Pops turned his head to me while we were perched on the comfortable, thick, wooden railings and said, "Thanks, kid. I needed this."

"Are you ready to go?"

He nodded. "Yeah. Yeah, I am."

I never did like being in jail, ever, but I Loved how it raised me to be at a better level. Thank you to all the women and men in blue. Thank you.

145

Audition at the Apollo

Before I tell you about my experience at The Apollo, I have to back up a bit and start from the County Colgate Country Singing Contest Randy had entered me in a year earlier. There were 20 of us in this contest, and the tech rehearsals went amazing. However, show time was rough. I swear I heard the live band behind me hit a few sour notes on purpose. But I clearly wasn't ready, either. I was a nervous mess.

I didn't win, but on the drive back to Fort Myers, it was drizzling and Randy was driving, so I turned on the radio and the Elvis Presley song, "Crying in The Chapel" was playing.

Without a beat, I spewed out, "That's the song I'm gonna sing at the Apollo."

"What's that?" Randy asked.

"Are you kidding me? You've never heard of the Apollo?"

"No. What is it?"

"It's only the greatest place to ever get the chance to sing! It's in New York City, in Harlem. I'm going there. Will you help me?"

"Of course!" Randy said. "I just never heard of the place."

"Boy, you really *have* been sheltered."

In the following weeks the audition was confirmed; so was my trip to the Apollo. Randy sent me alone to New York.

The audition was set for early in the morning. I was dressed warm. And stylish – with a big three-inch high heel – I was going through my high-heel phase. It was fun.

The line began to grow fast, I was about 20th in a line that was already swelling to hundreds.

And wouldn't you know it, I had to pee. So a woman I made friends with in line said she'd watch my spot.

When I returned from the McDonald's around the corner, the line was 40 people into the building already. I was being forced back toward the end of the line.

Unwilling to give up my rightful place in line, I went up to security on faith and said what had happened.

He looked at me and said, "I remember you. Go ahead, get in where you were."

Thank you, Jesus!

We were all seated on the second balcony awaiting our turn to audition. In groups of five we were led into a large white room with a piano in one corner and a microphone and stand in the middle. Four large speakers were placed around the room. Three judges sat on one side of the room, the five of us seated auditioners on the other side.

My turn came and I gave them a CD of my music. I sang for 30 seconds and was quickly scooted off stage.

My big chance… and I'd blown it. I just knew it.

"Come here," they said to me. "You got the gig. Come back on this date. Congratulations."

I couldn't believe it! But a little bit of me did.

In my heels, I ran down the stairs, past all the kids standing in line.

I marched straight up to the security guard who remembered me and told him I'd passed the audition.

"Way to go," he said to me.

We high fived each other, then I skipped across the street.

Suddenly I was frozen. I forgot where I was.

147

I was now looking at four large poster-size black-and-white photographs of naked black men hanging from trees, dead, while six black dudes dressed in long white robes hollered occasionally, "The white man is the devil... The white man is the devil!"

Giddy with my own triumph, I said to them, "Hi, guys! I just passed my audition at the Apollo."

They laughed at me, and said, "Get away from us."

I continued to skip away from them, then made it halfway up the block before I found a pay phone. I called Randy to tell him the good news.

We cried tears of joy together over the phone, as the six dudes behind me continued to cry out their own feelings.

Awaiting my Moment in the Spotlight at the Apollo

Back in Fort Myers, there was a six-month wait 'til show time at the Apollo. That gave me plenty of time to think up costuming ideas. I got this vision of a costume to perform in while singing "Crying in the Chapel." It was a priest's outfit with black stiletto high-heel boots. And wouldn't you know it, God sent me a seamstress to help make the outfit. Her name was Ruth, she had to be about 75, but she was the kindest woman ever. She was the mother of one of Randy's friends down the street. They were so nice to us... well, to him. I kept my distance from them for the most part, 'cause I was still on dope. No way was I going to come out and say, 'Hey, there! I'm smoking crack to fulfill a vision I had one time.' Let's face it, that's not exactly acceptable at *any* party – with or without alcohol.

Plus they had friends who work with the government in some capacity, and they told us once, "All our friends' background records are looked up because we're friends of government people."

I don't know, maybe they were blowing smoke up my ass, but they didn't seem the type of people to just say shit like that without any basis. It would be beneath them.

So now I had more reasons to be paranoid. But their Mum, Ruth, was good to me. We liked each other's company and her homemade breakfasts were the best. Ruth, I Love you and your beautiful family.

She made the costume, and off I went, ignoring everyone's pleas to not wear it – and I mean *everyone*. We planned for me to drive to Pittsburgh and pick up Randy at the airport. From there, I announced to all my past group homes and foster parents – even Mr. and Mrs. Heart – I was headed to the Apollo.

They all said "Good luck… and don't wear that costume." Every one of them.

My God, that line was getting old!

Finally, we arrived in New York City. We stayed in a hostel right next to Central Park to save money. Plus, it had been fun the last time I was there.

Randy wasn't too thrilled, but even he had to admit the price was dynamite. Randy isn't a tightwad, because given the choice between a hot dog or a steak, it's steak all day, and yes, I'm the hot dog, in more ways than one!

Early in the morning, I was in the basement, rehearsing the song, secluded from the upstairs breakfast room. A few dusty chairs and tables littered the room. I'd begun to sing and everything was going great.

But right when I reached the middle of the song, the Universe made its latest prediction. "You're gonna be booed off the stage."

Talk about a kick to the balls!

On my fourth attempt to finish the song, Randy arrived downstairs.

When the middle part was interrupted again, I lost it and kicked a few chairs over, startling the shit out of Randy – and me, truth be told.

"What the hell! What's going on?" Randy asked me.

For the next 10 seconds, I talked to God in my head. I asked, "Can I tell him? I mean about you predicting some crazy-ass future-telling shit. He's gotta know."

And the voice said, "Yes, I agree." Which, frankly, startled the hell out of me.

I looked at Randy, took a deep breath and said, "I'm getting booed off the stage tonight, right in the middle of the song, after that one note. I haven't sung past it yet this morning."

In the past, I'd told Randy about the voices I've heard. I believe his Love for his mom's Bible beliefs is the same and more with me in the same degree. He's never laughed at me, and I Love him for that.

"No, don't say that," Randy said, shaking his head.

I was this wild combination of sad and mad and really kind of freaked out by this time. So to get our minds off this shit, we went for a snowy walk in Central Park.

Randy's cell phone rang. As he answered it, I walked about 10 feet away, dropped to my knees in the snow and prayed, contemplating quitting with a few baby-ish tears in my eyes.

I said, "Dad what the fuck are you doin' to me?! Alright, alright, if I do this thing tonight, I need a peace of mind about all this."

In the snap of a finger, my head and heart were warmed. I had this feeling like taking a test and without ever seeing the results of the test, I knew I'd gotten an A. I wasn't afraid one bit anymore.

I said "Thanks" to Pops upstairs and got off my knees.

I started strutting, kind of like George Jefferson, over to Randy.

Noticing right away my attitude had taken a full 180, he said, "What's up with you?"

I told him what happened, and off we went to the show.

It was 2 p.m. All the contestants and our managers were in the audience at the Apollo, going over tech rehearsals. I hadn't brought out my costume yet. Randy was getting reprimanded for filming the inside of the theatre.

When my turn came to do a short run through, I went up on stage and ran the show. The live band didn't like me asking them to start at a specific time.

I was asking for a three metal-drum tap, then begin the beats. They didn't give a shit what I was asking for. But in the hours to come, I promise they would never forget me. Three times we tried to get it right, but eventually the stage manager interrupted us and yelled out, "Come on now, this ain't that difficult!"

I quickly responded, "Thank you! That's what I'm saying!"

My rehearsal ended immediately after that and we all left the building.

When we returned after 7 p.m. for showtime, they split the 15 of us into two groups, girls and guys. Guys changed on the fourth floor, girls on the third.

At first, while we were changing, the room was loud and fun. But as I finished changing into my outfit and heels, the room got quiet quickly… and no one would talk to me or make eye contact.

I could hear those guys across from the Apollo on the day of my audition again. "The white man is the devil, the white man is the devil."

We were all asked to come to the basement for a pep talk – and a rules and manners lesson.

Every single person gave me this *What are you dressed like that for?* look.

I didn't respond to any of those looks, but I will now. I'm a stage-theatre kinda guy and I figured the song called for a dramatic flair. Plus, as I already pointed out, I was going through my high-heels phase. Besides which, I really thought New York was gonna love it. I still do to this day.

I was like number 10 to go on stage, so Randy and I snuck up to the forbidden 5th floor and walked amongst the rafters to the edge and looked down on all the stage performers. Good thing they didn't catch us – 'cause if they did, we'd have been kicked out.

Then came my turn. I had the bad luck to be following the most light-skinned, voluptuous girl – who absolutely stole the audience's heart. I found out after the show, the audience was all college boys and alumni from

Alabama! I never stood a chance!

The emcee asked the audience to be kind to me, which I found odd, but I knew what he meant. I might have a few nuts in my blood, but I ain't stupid. I rubbed the iconic stump I believe was a piece of tree the white man hung black people from. That was weird kinda, I didn't feel worthy. I walked and stood center stage, raised my arms high, exposing my high heels. The whole audience gasped, I swear. I was going down. The band started late, of course.

A few women cheered for me the whole way, but the boos won the day.

I walked off the stage with my head not hanging one bit. The surrounding staff and security patted me on the back and said, "You did good, really."

Randy had this look of disbelief on his face.

I said to him, "Let's go."

I changed back into my street clothes, everything but the boots. I had to leave that place in style. And hell no, I didn't cry. Not yet.

As we walked through the cold slush on the sidewalk, trying to catch a cab. I called Mr. Heart, because he'd asked me to let him know the outcome. I told him I was booed off the stage. For some sick-ass reason, I felt it was something they wanted to hear. No, let me rephrase that: For some sick-ass reason, I enjoyed telling them I failed.

When we returned to Fort Myers, every mailbox it seemed, was plastered with images of Baby V, a contestant on American Idol. She was a mail-delivery courier from Fort Myers. So right off the bat, I was a loser, and she was the winner... and we had never even met.

I think something like three thousand people had gathered downtown by the water to meet and greet her during the show's run. Get this, she pulled up in a huge white yacht. This drove me crazy with jealousy.

Then it happened: She lost. I immediately began crying like a baby on Randy's shoulder. For Baby V, and

Darren Timothy Numer

for me.

Another Day, Another Audition... Cowboy Style

I was starting to get to know the stage life, all because of God, Randy, the Universe. I loved singing, and it was quickly becoming my life. So I set up an audition with the owner of a restaurant on Fort Myers Beach that allows live bands to play there. The audition was set for 3 p.m.

I brought Randy's Grandma's church hymnal and a cowboy outfit, complete with ten-gallon hat. Now there's a visual for you, huh?

I was going to sing, "Away in a Manger," and I carried into the restaurant a bale of hay, covered by a bed sheet to ensure no spills. The bale of hay was under my arm, cowboy boots on my feet. It was a beautiful day and I moseyed on into the restaurant's yellow dining room, surprising the hell out of the only two customers in the place.

I met the owner again, this small old Italian dude. He watched me set up, and stayed awhile.

He pointed toward one end of the room. "Get up on that small stage and do your thing."

So I got up there, and revealed my bale of hay. I was planning to portray a little boy who didn't want to practice his singing lesson. I opened the hymnal to the song, then looked over to the kitchen and began my surprise sketch performance.

I hollered, "I ain't coming out of this barn ever! And I ain't singing that song no more – you can't make me! Okay, I'll sing it one more time, and that's it!"

I looked down at the music and began to sing

"Away in a Manger."

It started off well, as far as I can remember, but I began to lose it when I looked out into the vast crowd of people who weren't there. Only this 50-year-old couple sitting next to each other, eating their Italian late lunch, facing me. She was eating spaghetti. I know this because when our eyes met, she was finishing slurping in her last bite. I mean she was doing some good sucking! This string of spaghetti was like seven feet long and she sucked it in one suck. Well that did it for me. I lost it.

This next part is true, too, unbelievable though it may be. I'm sure my nerves were getting the best of me. But what I saw next scared the shit out of me. I'd been singing for half a minute or so, trying to not look at my words, but I was losing it. I couldn't remember the words to the song. So for confidence and comfort, I looked down at the words. You won't believe it, because I don't believe it myself… but I'll say it anyway. The actual notes and words in this hymnal fell right off the pages, just like something you might see in a cartoon. I shit you not.

Wow, I thought, *the Universe does __not__ want me to get this gig, whatsoever!* That's what came to my heart. So I'm on stage, remembering not one word, and the more I moved the hymnal around, the more letters and notes fell off the pages.

My failure was loud. You could hear it in my voice, and in the new words I was making up. The couple stopped eating altogether, refusing to make eye contact with me now, too. I think they started praying I would shut up, but I couldn't, I had to see this through to the end. The owner rolled his eyes and gave a look of apology to his customers then hid behind a door.

I think I sang something about little baby Jesus catching a cab to New York. And I was done after that. I stayed on stage for like 10 minutes, waiting for the owner to come back and say, "Don't call us, we'll call you."

He never did. I finally ambled off the stage, heading

for the front door, refusing to look at the older couple's wounds that I inflicted. That's when I realized I must not have secured my bale of hay too well, because all over their newly mopped floor were bits of hay. Everywhere. I had left a big long trail! No wonder the owner was gone – he had to get a broom. Or a horse or half a dozen head of cattle or something. I gotta go back to that restaurant some day, I just gotta. LOL.

The Coral Building

While I was in Florida, a few years before I met Randy, I was hanging with these two girls, both named Jenny. We would wreak havoc on Fort Myers. Just your typical stupid, juvenile shit. For instance, we'd drive up to gas stations, fill our cars and drive away without paying.

One day, in a mood to make mischief, we came upon this giant coral-colored building. Maybe three stories tall, almost square in shape with no windows, except the glass double-door entryway. Earlier that day we'd accidentally broken a lamp outside a huge church while we were playing on it. Then the girls took my picture (using our newly stolen Polaroid camera) on a hill with boxer shorts over my head. When I saw the picture, I got mad and demanded they give it back. In my mind, I always thought one day I might get to tell about this but I wanted to control any pictures of me out there.

But back to the building. It looked abandoned, so we decided it was suddenly our calling in life to trash the place, leave our mark. We walked up to the front doors and, to our surprise, one of them was unlocked.

Inside, it wasn't dirty, like you'd expect for an abandoned building; it resembled an empty hallway of a courthouse. There were stairs to our right, and a door to somewhere. We walked in, looking to destroy anything. I was the last to go in.

From the moment I stepped inside, something just didn't feel right.

I hollered at them both, "Stop! Let's get out of here, this place gives me the creeps."

It was like the building was telling me, *"If you do anything to this place, you'll regret it. Now leave."*

I said, "Come on, girls. This place, it's off limits to us." And we ran out.

Fast forward a bunch of years. The Jennys were "spitting out babies" and "staying away from this faggot" – their words and their rules. Understandable though, being gay or having gay friends wasn't exactly popular back then.

Meanwhile, I was starting to grow more confident in my relationship with Randy; and in other news, I felt I was ready to be in a stage play.

Randy had said to me, "Darren, I love that you wash our underwear, and cook and clean, but what do you *really* want to do with your life?"

I thought about it for a while, then I said, "I wanna entertain people. I know I can do a good job at it."

That was good enough for Randy. Without my knowledge, he scheduled an audition for me the following Saturday morning with the Fort Myers Beach Orpheus Theatre Group.

After my cold-read audition, the director, Miss Donna P. went behind a curtain and I heard her whisper loudly, "He's perfect! I want him in the play."

I played the lawyer Barnett Lloyd in the stage play, "Crimes of the Heart." Got paid, too. That was different and cool. So now I was a professional stage actor!

I'd like to tell you about Sheryl Rupert. A beautiful blonde, blue-eyed bombshell, maybe 40 years old, she was in our group of actors; shortly after I joined the Orpheus group, she hired me as her personal driver, due to chronic back pain. She also had scoliosis, but hers was much more severe than mine. She was one of the unlucky ones who hadn't gotten treatment for her condition. Sheryl didn't believe I had scoliosis, until I showed her the long scars on my shins. We were besties from then on.

As for the rest of the group (except Amanda P. whom I had a schoolboy crush on, to me she was beautiful and the most talented actress)... well, I kinda had a falling out with them; and regrettably, I took out my hostilities on Lucy, a beautiful, sweet, red-headed actress.

I had been with the Orpheus Group for maybe a year. So of course I was certain I was ready to write and direct my own stuff, with no background skills to back up my work. To everyone else in the theatre group, I must have seemed like a toddler asking for the keys to the truck. One week they would support my stage adaptation of the movie, *Walking Across Egypt*, by Clyde Edgerton. Then the next week, they'd discourage me. Again, except Amanda. She kept saying, "Go for it!"

This went on for about six months, 'til the play took off with two of the Orpheus players in the cast. Doc was one of them and Lucy was the other.

Oh! I forgot: Mark L., our other director, made me the lead in a reading stage performance of *The Hitchhiker's Guild to the Galaxy*, written by Douglas Adams. That alone blew my ego up!

After the second performance of our show, I was down with a bad case of the flu and Lucy was staying at our place.

Randy was drunk and egging me on about my still having a beef with the Orpheus group. It was about 1 a.m. and I was ranting about Lucy (who was in the bedroom next to ours).

I blurted out, "She's only in this fucking play 'cause she ain't doing nothing else. If she had a better gig, she'd dump us in a heartbeat. She don't give a fuck about us!"

There's no way Lucy couldn't have heard what I'd said. Right afterward, she called a friend to pick her up, then went outside.

I wanted to go out to where she stood at the end of the driveway, waiting. I wanted to take back those horrible things I had said, but I couldn't. I didn't just hurt Lucy,

I'd stabbed our friendship in the heart.

Meanwhile, Sheryl was wanting me to grow as a performer, so she had me audition for a new play she was in. It was at this theatre I'd never heard of or even seen, or so I thought. The play was *Man of La Mancha,* written by Mitch Leigh and Dale Wasserman.

We pulled up to this building and it was big, kinda square, with no windows, and it was the color of coral. It was that same building that told me to leave a few years earlier. This 'talking' building was the Cape Coral Community Theatre. Today I believe it's named the Cultural Park Theatre. And this time it looked like I'd be allowed to stay.

I passed my audition. When it was over I asked to go up to the back of the audience row of seats. I had to see that spot where I once stood and had gotten a verbal spanking from this building.

Three years later Sheryl Rupert passed away from a brain hemorrhage. The pain in her back had made it to her brain. R.I.P. Sheryl, and thank you for lifting me up.

Sheryl, you too had told me to go to Hollywood… Guess what, Babe? I made it!

Cover Art, Explained

Now I want to explain why I chose this cover art. That tattoo is on my inner arm. I got it to hide my chicken-shit, weak-ass suicide attempt. Well, I didn't actually want to kill myself; I just wanted to show Randy how nuts I was going on this crack cocaine shit.

We had come home from a night of booze and friends. I waited for Randy to pass out so I could steal his wallet to go get high. Wait, that's not exactly true. This was how the drug treated me.

We'd go to bed and I would fall asleep with him, but within an hour I would wake up, completely sober and in a zombie-like state, talking to God every time.

This time, Randy woke up and stopped me from going anywhere. But I wasn't having it. So we began to wrestle. I could feel the drug pulling me by the hair, just aching to get a fix. I was ready to end it. I ran into the kitchen and grabbed the biggest knife I could find. I turned toward Randy with the knife in my hand.

Randy laughed at me, asking, "What, you gonna use that on me?"

I said, "No, don't you get it? I don't wanna be on this fucking drug anymore. I would hurt myself before you, ever."

Then it happened, I figured if he wasn't convinced, I would just have to show him. I began – the only way I can explain it is "chopping broccoli" on my left inner arm, a good six slices.

Yup, I had his full attention now.

The blade burned with each swift strike. The blood started coming out of the slices one at a time, in order, then it wouldn't stop coming.

Randy took the knife out of my hand. He looked me in the eyes with compassion and said, "Come on, get that under the sink."

I recoiled from his request. "*Now* do you fucking believe me?"

I ran out the door, dripping red dots everywhere. I was a little bit hoping he'd come after me. I ran two houses down and passed out on our neighbor's loose brown-pebbled driveway. I remember that because some of the pebbles got lodged in my cuts when I came to a few minutes later.

The blood had stopped. I got mad at that – and the fact that Randy hadn't even come after me. I lay there a while longer, hoping I wasn't giving some insomniac neighbor a show... but if I was, I might as well ham it up.

I crawled to my knees, then to a stand. Walked home, sad as can be. Went in the house only to hear Randy snoring in his bedroom, already passed out again. Gee, buddy, thanks.

For the next year and a half, I wore long-sleeve shirts all the time. In Florida. I had to. Once I forgot and went to the store in a T-shirt. When this cashier gave me my change back, I turned my arm over to receive my change. The girl looked at the fresh red scars, hard. She couldn't take her eyes off them. Her jaw dropped half an inch right in front of me. Then, in slow motion, she looked at me and blinked once, proceeding to give me the saddest eyes ever. I felt humiliated as all get out.

A year and a half later, the scar was still visible and I was sick of long-sleeve shirts in the Florida heat.

One Saturday morning I fulfilled a short-term dream: getting a tattoo to cover those fucking scars. I drove an hour and fifteen minutes north of town. I didn't want to live anywhere near my tattoo artist's town.

In a small purple plaza on the right I found a tattoo place. There was a girl and a young guy opening shop. The guy came over to me.

The first thing out of my mouth was, "Can I talk to you outside?"

He said, "Sure."

When we got outside, I rolled my sleeve up and showed him what I needed covered. I had 60 bucks on me so I was just going to get, in black letters, 'Mummy,' spelled sideways.

He said, "No, you'll still be able to see the scar under the black ink. May I draw you a suggestion?"

"Yes, please."

An hour and a few tears later, I had my new tattoo, and I was wearing a T-shirt. I called Randy and woke him up.

I said, "Get ready, Randy, a new Darren's coming home. Thanks to Mummy."

Worst (But Most Deserved) Ass-Kicking Ever!

Around that same time in my life, I received my worst ass kicking ever. Generally, I'm a Lover not a fighter, preferably. But I was 100% in the wrong. It was 1 a.m. and I was in Pine Manor, the bad side of town in Fort Myers, and I was up to no good.

Randy was passed out at home in bed. I was in a big brown Ford F150 truck getting pulled over by a police officer and thinking, *Jail, here I come again.*

I pulled into the neighborhood where the drugs were sold (and where I'd first met Randy, come to think of it). A short, muscular, handsome cop asked me to get out of the truck. He began asking me questions whose answers I couldn't care less about. I was too busy staring down the street, wondering how far could I get before he caught me. So I took off.

I heard him behind me say, "Ah shit, he's a runner!"

I was already two houses down the road, but he was kinda catching up. I turned left at the fourth house and found myself facing a seven-foot wooden gate. I flew up that thing so fast, then the descent was scary. Seven feet takes awhile to get down.

The cop was right behind me. I was blocked in this fenced-in backyard, and I could hear the neighborhood dogs all around me, barking. Then, *Bam!* I got knocked to the ground from behind.

This cop was on me and not letting go. I kinda liked it but I didn't tell him that.

The night was young (well, relatively speaking) and I had energy to spare, so I decided to see whether I could play possum under him. So I lay as still as I could and he loosened up on me.

I booked out from under him somehow and flew up that gate again… and doooown again. I ran past some bushes in front of the house whose gate I'd just jumped. I went to the other side of the house.

That gate was *way* higher, so I went and hid under the bushes. It actually was a good place to hide and rest, as I was getting tired fast. From under the bushes, I watched as the officer ran past a few times, baffled, I'm sure.

What did I do? I took a nap… only to be awakened less than 10 minutes later by a platoon of angry fire ants crawling up my shorts. I'd fallen asleep on their ant-hill.

I wanted to yell out, but couldn't, because now there were four squad cars pulling up, and it looked like all male officers. It was time to surrender. Plus, I felt they knew I was there. They began gathering closer toward me.

I crawled out and said, "Here I am."

Out came a few of their guns. They ordered me to stay on the ground.

I wasn't about to argue with them there. But I had already run away from them once – no wait, twice – so yeah, I can see where they might get a little excited and draw weapons.

Then the beatings began. I swear I could hear "Time To Say Goodbye" by Andrea Bocelli and Sarah Brightman in my heart as it began.

All six officers began to pile on top of me, and started kicking in my ribs. They were stabbing into my spine with their knees and night sticks and kicking the back of my head. I swear I saw three of them drooling like wild dogs. If I had been a piece of steak earlier in the day, I was complete and utter meatloaf by the end of this night.

They avoided hitting my face, I noticed, but they

didn't mind grinding it into the ground, that was for sure. Hey, who needs rouge when you've got asphalt?

This went on for a good while, until an unexpected hero showed up. I never in my life thought I'd welcome diarrhea. I couldn't help it. Earlier that day at a gay bar named the O.P. (Office Pub), they'd held a chili contest.

I went limp all over again and waited for the smell to hit their nostrils. It took thirty seconds. I know because I counted while they kept kicking me. It was as if we were all in an elevator and you know how when it was you who farted, and you hope the doors would open before anyone noticed? Well these doors weren't opening. One by one, they began peeling off of me like a withered onion, pinching their noses and gagging... screaming, "Ah, man! What's that *smell?*"

It was me.

I had to turn my head because I started laughing. Seriously, what else could I do?

Then this weird sense of boldness came over me. I don't know why I acted this way, but I started chastising the officers. "What the fuck is wrong with you guys? I'm half your size, and already on the ground. Yet the need to beat the shit out of another human being is all you can think about?"

Nobody said a word.

Then, I went way below the belt. "Wait, I know what kind of guys you are: You're the kind of guys who beat their wives when no one's looking."

Still, none of them said a word. I'd struck a nerve on that one, I could feel it. The place went silent and still after that statement. It kinda scared me, I felt I was right about a few of them and the others knew it, too. You see, when you catch a thief red handed, they tend to laugh or smirk. But when you bust in on an abuser, they go silent. Name of the game, I guess.

That night we all got busted; I just got the shittier end of the stick.

A Different Way of Getting High

Wanna go for a ride? I'll take you. I learned how to fly a plane. I did. Remember Ruth, the lady who made my priest outfit for the Apollo performance? Well, her daughter and son-in-law are a big part of the reason I learned to fly. Her son-in-law was a pilot himself... and if you've ever heard the expression, "You are who you associate with," you'll know why I'm a firm believer in that. Which is also why, to this day, I choose my friends wisely!

These were mostly Randy's friends, but I was in the mix by association. His friends are real cool, they work hard and play hard.

Randy had just hooked me up with a job three hours north, as a superintendent overseeing a tire store being built. Somewhat reluctantly they allowed Randy to hire me for this gig. Before this, the last time I'd been on a construction site I was just an assistant, a helper. Nothing bigger than that.

But they made a deal with Randy. "We'll pay twelve -hundred a week and you'll pay the taxes in the end. Or we'll pay a thousand a week and we'll pay the taxes."

Holy shit! I'd never made this kind of money, ever! We took the latter choice.

With that much money, I asked Randy if I could learn to fly; it would cost a hundred bucks per lesson, once a week. There was a small airport around the block from the construction site.

So on my lunch breaks every Wednesday, I was up

in the air, flying a Cessna.

A wonderful memory that goes with this was I'd picked up one of those celebrity magazines, and I read that Brad Pitt was learning to fly, too. Who could have guessed I'd have something in common with Brad Pitt?!

My flight instructor was my age (30 something), but he had the demeanor of a special-ed teacher – which made all the difference for me. But this one time (and thank God it was only once!) my regular instructor was out for the day. My substitute instructor was a Marine sergeant type of guy – a big, tall, older white dude with a military-style haircut.

Now, before you take off in a plane, it is absolutely mandatory you crawl all over that plane doing a full body check – and check the fuel. I barely got through that part with this Marine guy watching over me. As we squished together into the plane, he barked at me every 10 seconds. While we were in the air, if I'd been wearing a parachute, I would have jumped out.

To be honest, the things he said to me were loud and beautiful. He convinced me to get my pilot's certificate, and then quickly find another hobby. Flying is fun, but can never be taken lightly. And I was. Taking it lightly, that is. I was still on drugs, and showing up to my lessons hung over at times. It wasn't right of me to do so. In the time it took to build the garage, I got my daytime flight certificate. Randy came up to watch me take my solo flight test.

I passed, despite one big bouncy landing. After your successful flight test, you autograph a T-shirt, which they staple to the walls in their office.

I signed mine *Dagwood*. I've never flown since then, and the world smiled.

During this time I became friends with Charrie Gibson when she moved in next door at the duplex on the bay water. She was a schoolteacher, so of course you know I fell in love with her immediately. We both smoked and cussed like sailors straight off a battleship. And we formed a brother-and-sister bond like Gorilla Glue. Years later, after I moved to California, she came to visit, and this is what happened. You see, I had never told anyone I was on crack, until...

I was terrified I had lost my friend when I failed to pick her up at the airport for her visit to Los Angeles. She would be the only one, besides my husband while I was on crack cocaine, to whom I confessed it was a vision I'd had and I would be off the drug at a certain point in time.

I was high as a kite when I was supposed to pick up Charrie at the airport. Paranoid as all hell, I approached LAX, drove over to the Westin and called my friend as she was exiting the plane. I mentioned to her I was sure I would get arrested if I went through the LAX security. So Charrie met me at the Westin. I was so messed up, visibly reacting to the crack cocaine, I asked her to drive my van. As she drove, I confessed my vision and sins to her. I also told her I'd one day tell my story out loud to the world, but I had to go through this, and I was unable to deny that truth. She began to cry as she dropped herself off at her motel. Completely humiliated and embarrassed by my actions, I did not visit her until years later. However a true friend does not let you down when you're on the ground.

Years have passed since that day, the vision made its full circle and to this day I am still very good friends with my Charrie. Much love to her and her daughter, our goddaughter, Andromeda.

In case you're wondering how the building of the garage went, I came in second-fastest garage built – ever – for this particular brand. But not because I knew what the hell I was doing.

I was sweating profusely on my first day when the foundation guys surrounded me with blueprint questions. They knew I didn't know shit about construction. Every time they'd ask me a question about the construction site, my go-to answer was, "Let's get Randy on the line," which he, himself, had suggested from the get go. *Thank you, Randy.*

I had a love-hate relationship with that job. I loved being there; the crew hated me. When the tall block walls were finished, someone stuck a glove on top of the rebar, giving me the middle finger. I shut the whole works down 'til they removed it. That took a full rainy day. They hated me more after that.

They even knocked over the shitter. That little prank took two days to get fixed... and it allowed me the opportunity to make a new enemy with the owner of that porta john company, too. My job duty was mostly to stay in the job-site trailer, answer the phone and walk around to check on the workers here and there.

When I returned from lunch about two months into this gig, my Hooters calendar was missing and my mini sledgehammer paperweight was gone. After that, I kept the trailer locked. By then, the concrete guys who had given me the most hell were finally gone, which made finishing up more fun and easy. Around the same time we were finishing up the job, Randy's bosses went back on their word about paying our taxes. So he paid the taxes and then quit.

171

The Engagement

Randy and I got engaged at Christmastime. I still don't know why. He's a diamond, I'm a lump of coal.

On Christmas morning, we exchanged gifts. Afterward, he said to me, "There's one more gift. Look on the mantel."

There she was, that distinct little box. I knew what it was. Hell I had to, I'd been hounding him for a ring all year long. It seems it was the popular thing at the time for gay couples all over America. Still is today.

I couldn't open the box. He had to do it for me. I was stunned and thought, *Does this guy know what he's doing? He must be nuts for wanting to marry me!*

Randy opened the box, showing off a beautiful light-gold band and five cut diamonds. He took it out and placed it on my finger. He asked, "Will you be mine?"

I said, "I never wasn't. Yes, I'm all yours."

Then we kissed and cried together.

Later that night we returned from the clubs and I wanted to get high, as usual. Thankfully, that night Randy let me take out my frustrations on the Christmas tree. When I was finished, the poor thing remained as a visual reminder for me to see how ridiculous I was being. So I went to bed peaceful. That was rare.

The following morning, the Florida sun came shining through our light-yellow curtains, revealing glittering broken Christmas ornaments all over the yellow-and-orange terrazzo living-room floor.

The tree was broken in half, with 60 percent of its branches on the ground. The scent of pine needles was everywhere. So were the needles themselves! The only thing holding the tree together were the twinkling lights. They had somehow survived.

After that was all cleaned up, we sat down and talked about marriage. I said to him I really don't feel like marriage is as important as it's all set up to be. Did I want the ring? Yes, but not for the outward reasons. I don't give a shit about diamonds. I think I can speak for the majority when I say I just want to Love someone and to be Loved right back. We humans have forced a mineral from earth to prove that point, when we truthfully should rise above our earthly possessions. We will in time; I feel it.

Randy agreed fully.

I said to him, "You're a Casanova, and me too, sometimes. So if you need to get it on out there, just don't do it in front of me, and I won't do it in front of you."

We kissed on it and then exchanged the engagement ring for a hot tub for the backyard one week later... which went beautifully with the above-ground swimming pool I put in when Randy went home to Texas to visit his folks.

He'd rented me a backhoe to keep me busy. It did. In the backyard was also a 7,000-gallon fish pond with Plexiglas sidewalls for viewing the fish. It was amazing to look at, and took four years to build.

When we moved to California a few years later, we decided to rent out that house on Burtwood Ave. That meant we had to demolish the pond, the pool and the spa for liability reasons. But we had so much fun in that backyard... we threw the best parties!

An Open Letter to Florida

Dear Florida,

I miss you. Didn't think I'd ever say those words. But I mean 'em, every part.

Thank you for your warm, heavy rains to help me wash away my tears. You held me down when I couldn't stop shaking. You put sand under my feet and salt on my tongue. You showed me a keyhole in the Universe. I got hooked in you with no regrets.

You fed me freedom and thought. You fed me pickles and tickles. I enjoyed your wind through my hair. I Loved meeting people who had the color of your sky in their eyes.

I can still feel your tide all through the hours. Your still demeanor and your soft hills dance slowly in memory.

Over my heart is my hand that holds you close to me. *(Okay, that last one there was even too much for me.)* Hey, Florida, Love ya Baby. xoxoxo

A Tribute to Tiny Jesus (or T.J. for Short)

(This next story I dedicate to Tiny Jesus, may you Rest in peace. Blood cancer took him down in less than five years. Love you, T.J. Who's Tiny Jesus? Come read and find out.)

How about one more Florida story before we head west to L.A.? This, just like the others, has to be rewound just a little bit. But this time I don't mind reliving this story. It had to be done. However, there was a severely injured party.

I finally wanted a dog again, after a year or two of grieving over Bo. Not just any dog, this time, I prayed for an English Mastiff. If you're unfamiliar with that breed of dog, it's one of the biggest dogs around. Their colors range from fawn and apricot to brindle. My puppy was a $600 fawn pup. Randy watched me save up money for him. We named him Tiny Jesus.

Yeah, I was still on drugs at the time, but I gave Randy the money to hold onto, so I wouldn't mess up and do drugs with it. It took me almost a year to save that much.

Everyone was in love with Tiny Jesus. He was so calm and kind. Our next-door neighbor, a 12-year-old girl, loved taking him on walks around the neighborhood.

Like all my other pets, he went everywhere with me… to the store, the park, the beach, everywhere. He was lovely and Loved.

When Tiny was about two years old, I had left the front door open. While I was on the phone with a friend, in walks Tiny, dragging his left back foot on the ground, his skin barely holding everything together. He must have been in shock, 'cause he wasn't showing any type of pain or stress. He just casually limped to the back bedroom. I hung up the phone and started hollering for Randy to come quick.

He rushed in from the backyard. "What?"

"It's Tiny; he's been hurt bad."

We went to where Tiny lay and saw his leg bone had clearly been dragged across the asphalt by a car. It made a one-inch separation of his shin bone. It looked like fresh hamburger with a filed-down chicken bone.

I lost it.

Randy said to me, "Darren, go get some wet hot towels."

I did as he instructed and Randy wrapped him up.

We loaded Tiny – all 145 pounds of him – onto the back of our truck and rushed to the animal hospital. He ended up having to stay there for about two months for proper care and healing.

Tiny came out wonderful, cast and all. He had his cast on for a good while. And I could totally relate to what he was going through in that cast!

When it came off, he was back to his old self; but he never left the house on his own again.

The morning after Tiny's injury, I hopped on my bicycle to look for blood marks on the streets. I rode all around and didn't find a thing.

In time, Tiny was doing well, but there was this red Ferrari constantly speeding down our street. Constantly. I eventually found out the driver lived only three blocks away from our place. And I wanted to send that guy a message. But to get the full impact of what I did, I need to back up to when I was living with the Hearts, way back when.

We kids were playing football in the street one day, when two cars came speeding around the bend toward us.

We heard two loud car tire screeches up the road. Mr. Lock, one of the kids' dads, yelled to us to get out of the street. He himself picked up two of the younger kids for a rescue.

We got out of the way just in time, as the first car flew by. The second one was approaching quickly. Mr. Lock took the almost-full fruit-juice bottle he was drinking from and threw it at the windshield of the car as it went flying by. The plastic bottled smashed open, covering the car with red juice. The girl driving hit the brakes, but didn't stop. Turned out, this girl and her boyfriend were playing Speed Racer with each other, down our Dallett Road.

The cops were called, the parents screamed. We kids ran to the end of the street to measure the skid marks they had left on the street as they made their turn, prior to almost killing us all. In my mind it must have been like a thousand feet.

No one went to jail over the incident and the neighbors grew tighter.

So back to this speeding red Ferrari pissing me off. I didn't have any fruit juice, but I did have a cement block… and knew just what to do with it.

Early that following Sunday morning, when no one was up, I grabbed a red bandana, a cement block and a one-page letter I'd written, and rode my bicycle to that Ferrari driver's home. There she was, parked in the grass crooked like a show off, sweating the morning dew.

Carefully, not dropping the cement block, I pulled up close to the car. I put the block down on the ground and got off my bike. I opened the bandana fully and lay it on the hood of the car. Then I took the letter and placed it on top of the bandana. Last, I picked up the cement block and gingerly placed it atop the letter and the bandana, making not a scratch.

I got back on my bike and rode away, laughing to myself, thinking this guy's gonna trip when he reads that letter. The letter went like this: "Dear neighbor, we have kids and pets playing in our streets. So, the next time you come flying down our street... well, you know the rest. Have a great day."

Hooray for Hollywood

Months before we ever thought of moving to California, Randy asked me where should we go to let me entertain, New York or California. My relations with New York were not the best, so you know the answer to that one!

Randy looked up the best construction companies in L.A. Then he set up an interview, just like that. The very first place he picked not only flew him out to California for an interview, they hired him – and paid to move all our household belongings out there, too. We were like, Holy shit, this is going fast. And it was.

We'd just finished up with the Apollo in New York. The next item on our list was west of the Mississippi, and to complete our new stage play, after getting permission from a relative of Enid Bagnold, who wrote the novel, *National Velvet*. We were about to write the stage version of it.

Randy wanted me to go out to California for six months, to get established. Then we'd switch places. I'd go back to Florida and get the house packed up and meet him in California six months later-ish.

Unbelievable. Just unbelievable! The drug was still in me, as far as I knew; yet I was about to drive to California in a sweet 10-year-old white Mercedes station wagon – with a sunroof. I'm *nuts* for a sunroof!

So off I went, across the United States of America. I did like my brother Billy told me many years ago: I stayed mostly in the right-hand lane and cruised the whole way.

I traveled up the 75 Highway to the 10 Highway. Where the views were indescribable? I don't remember… because I didn't really look at them. I only had my eye on the prize. I do remember the left side of Texas taking forever to cross. New Mexico had those beautiful orange, yellow and tan mountain rocks all around, I think.

Still, I couldn't get to California fast enough. In Arizona I switched to Highway 8; that put me toward San Diego. It was early morning when I got to San Diego. And it took like four hours to get from there to L.A.

There she was! I could see immediately a full mix of different colored people. My people, we're the people who Love people. It's that simple.

I got off of exit 8-C which dropped me on Gower Road straight into Hollywood, down onto Hollywood Blvd. with my peeps. I made that right-hand turn onto the most-famous street in the world. And there they were, to my right and left, those stars stuck in a sidewalk. I had to see them up close right away!

I pulled over to the next available space and got out and saw their pretty little faces. I don't recall the names I was looking at, but I was impressed by how they looked. The stars looked like light-rose terrazzo outlined in gold. I know it isn't gold, but it looks like it. Really pretty. In the middle is a flat metal medallion depicting the star's craft. If you were an actor, there'd be happy- and sad-looking theatre masks. If you were a singer, there would be an old timey-looking microphone. And many more. Under the medallions was the artist's name in gold again. Each star is centered in its own two-foot by two-foot square. And the surface outlining the stars is slightly bumpy, grey and black with specks of shiny diamonds here and there. Top shelf all the way.

When I get my star, I want a book, the happy/sad masks *and* a microphone below my name.

I've been waiting to tell you this: I *love* directing stage plays.

About two or three years back in Florida, the first day of rehearsals in my first professional play, I watched my director, Miss Donna P., like a hawk. I was 33, and the light bulb in my head finally turned on. I knew what I wanted to be in life: a director of life!

At the time, I just wanted to be a stage director. That last thought just fell out of my head. Oops, a Freudian slip maybe? However I was completely mesmerized by how her actors followed her every move. How sure of herself she was and how comfortable she seemed with herself! I truly never knew there was a job out there like that – and I wanted in, fast! Thank you, Miss Donna P., you thrilled me so!

So I was in LaLa Land. I decided I didn't need to do the tourist thing. I've got the rest of my life to do that. Time to go see if there's room at the hostel.

I got a room to myself that first night, thank you, God.

In the morning I went to pay my bill for one more night and guess who I ran into in the lobby. My most-favorite cartoon creature in the world: Spongebob Square Pants. Now if that wasn't a sign from above that I was in the right place, well then I just don't know nothin'!

He was my height, and passed right by me, then out the door.

I was in such shock I had to ask the clerk at the desk, "Was that Spongebob that just left?"

"Yup," the clerk replied, as if it were a question he answered all the time. "He lives here. Every day that guy puts on that costume and cruises on Hollywood Boulevard, posing in pictures with the tourists for money."

I was just blown away. I would stay there only one more day. I decided I had to get away from that hostel. The people who stayed there seemed stuck. No, not stuck... more like they were comfortable not furthering themselves.

That second day, I drove down along Melrose and

noticed a Hollywood movie production being set up at the Improv Comedy Club. So I pulled over, went right up to the front door and asked who was in charge of this movie set and did they have work available. The gentleman in charge said no, however his friend was filming at a location three hours away if I was up for it.

Hell yeah! Second day in Hollywood and I got a job already. Too awesome!

Randy found me a room for rent in Hancock Park, just on the cusp of these huge mansions.

I've heard to get on a film crew you sometimes have to work for nothing – even as a laborer, which I was... and I did. It sucked, but I did what I had to do.

I met my new boss, a film director in the Valley. It's on the other side of the mountains from Hollywood, hot as hell in the summertime. He was wrapping up on an office-type film. I was there all day – from 5 a.m. until 8 p.m. I carried and stretched out hundreds of feet of thick electrical cords, learning quickly what each one did.

I was a sponge, taking in info, spouting out as many questions aloud. The director liked me and I got the gig with their next location, three hours away. That turned out to be a two-day gig, and I was appointed gopher boy. Which meant, go for this and go get that. I did that for more than 12 hours a day. When it came time to get paid at the end of the two-day shoot, I was offered a beer and a twenty-dollar pay check. So I went into their cooler, took two more beers and never called them back, or answered their calls. Holy shit, welcome to Hollywood.

Misunderstanding at the Improv

What do you do when you've been jolted by your first job in Hollywood? You head straight back to the source who got you the gig. So I went over to that comedy club, the Improv, intending to give that guy a few words about his film-director friend.

When I pulled up to the club around 11 a.m., no one was there. That film crew was gone. *Damn! I had something to say and no one to say it to!*

Someone came out the front door, walked through the small parking lot and into another door leading to... where? I didn't know. But I was about to find out.

For some reason I wanted to be a part of this club. So I thought *Let's see if they're hiring waiters.*

I followed that person through that door. When I opened it, I was presented with a tall staircase, which I climbed, then made a hard right U-turn to an L-shaped hallway. At the end of the hallway was a tiny little old white lady, busy at her desk, talking on the phone in her office while eating something. She had an impeccable style and the thickest eyelashes I'd ever seen. She looked like she was letting two black caterpillars nap on her eyelids.

I stood in front of her, waiting for her to notice me and talk to me.

Then she looked up, ended her conversation on the phone. She said, "Can I help you?"

"Yes, ma'am. I was wondering where do I go to apply for a job here?"

"You're in the wrong building," she barked at me almost with heart. "Go downstairs to the main building and go through the double doors and ask for Bob. He'll take care of you."

I thanked her with a smile and, to my surprise, she smiled back.

I went to see Bob and, without even having to fill out an application, I was being interviewed in the main comedy room, with all its black tables and chairs and the stage.

Bob asked a bunch of questions, and ended with one last question. "Why do you want to work here?"

I had nothing to lose, so I told the truth. "I wanna be close to that stage."

"Well, okay," he said.

We stood up together and shook hands. Then he looked me straight in the eyes and said, "Don't call us, we'll call you."

I'll never forget that. I then said gleefully, "Thank you! Thank you Bob."

I left that building so happy, knowing what he just said to me. I got the job, because, he said he's gonna call me. See I didn't have a clue that those words in Hollywood – don't call us, we'll call you – mean you *didn't* get the gig. But, like I said, I didn't know that at the time. For some reason, I felt the need to say a big thanks to caterpillar lady upstairs. I would never have gotten the job that I never did get, if it hadn't been for her.

I flew up those stairs, made those turns to her place and there she was again, eating something, while talking on the phone.

Only this time I had to wait like 10 minutes 'til she finally hung up the phone.

"Yessss? What can I do for you now?" she asked with a 'what do you want, kid?' demeanor.

I said to her, "I know you're busy, I just wanted to thank you for pointing me in the right direction. I got with

Bob and I think everything went well."

"Oh really?" she asked. "What did he say?"

"He said don't call us, we'll call you."

She did a small spit take and chuckled.

I said to her, "Thanks a lot, you have a great day." I stuck out my hand to shake her tiny little lady hand.

She shook my hand with her cute crooked fingers, and said, "You're welcome."

A small miracle was about to happen and I could smell it the moment these seven words came out of her mouth.

"Sit down, kid. Where are you from?"

That took my breath away. I could feel her wanting me, and I won't lie here, I wanted her. You know me and old people. I fucking Love 'em.

I sat down and answered her questions. Have you ever made a best friend in an elevator just in one minute? That's what was happening to me with this chick. I felt I could tell her any of my secrets and she'd still Love me. Yeah I used the word Love, and why shouldn't we?

I knew exactly where we were going with this conversation when she asked if I had a car and a valid driver's license. I actually had just gotten my driver's license back after a six-month suspension in Florida. But I didn't tell her that, yet.

"Yes, ma'am, I do."

"Call me Fran. What's your name?"

"Darren. Darren Numer. Nice to meet you again."

She said she needed a new driver to take her to and from work and also to do some errand runs on the side.

"When do I start?"

"Tonight. Can you be here to pick me up at 4 o'clock?"

"Yes, ma'am – oops I mean, yes, Fran. I'll see you soon."

I left my new friend and boss in her office, happy as a flying skylark with worms in his beak.

At four o'clock I picked her up to take her home and found out her cousin owns all the Improv Comedy Clubs around the world. You see, in Hollywood, it isn't only what you know, it's who you know. And I had just hit the jackpot. Holy shit, welcome to Hollywood!

Disappointing Fran

California served up some damn good crack cocaine, and I couldn't get enough of it. In the six months I stayed there before switching with Randy, I would be driving my own personal Miss Daisy, my Fran, to work during the day, then every other three weeks I was out getting high. The drug would work like that in me. After a few days of being on the drug, I'd be sobering up from the drug. I was kinda able to fight the inevitable drug addiction's pull for three weeks, typically, but not much more than that. At the end of a three-week sobriety stint, my time-punching drug card duty would scream at me till the card was punched. I didn't really know why I was doing the drug, but I did feel I was doing it a bit because I didn't have the courage to commit suicide. Actually, I did it because I was scared to live. Plus, the vision I had been given was real, as far as I knew. So in my heart I was truly waiting patiently for the drug's hold on me to end. But not so fast, because like I said, California was serving thick-ass steaks, and I was still hungry.

So of course it was inevitable that my Fran would discover my secret.

It happened one morning when I went to pick her up after a night of "all-you-can-eat steak." My regular mannerisms were as far away as possible, and she picked up on it fast.

When she was seated in the car next to me, as we drove, she remained huddled away from me. Nor did we speak much – and we had always talked. We never put the radio on in the car, not once. This was maybe a month or two since I'd started working for her.

That afternoon, when I went to pick her up, I confessed I was a drug addict.

She said, "I know. My son, who passed away about five years ago, was one too. He died homeless."

At the moment she told me that, I immediately felt like I was in front of this woman all because her son in heaven must have been guiding me to her.

Then she said, "Don't you ever do that to me again, I won't go through that ever again."

But I did, at least two more times. And I refused to pick her up a few other times because I was so messed up. She was forced to call a cab those times – even in the rain – twice. She forgave me every time. I feel she recognized the battle wasn't between us, but more within me.

She was begging for a happy ending this time around. So was I.

I didn't know who her son was, at first... until she peeled back the layers of history for me. Her son, Glenn Cowan, had been a pivotal player in healing the relationship between China and America, back when China wasn't allowing Americans in their country back in the '70s. He was the reason for the "Ping Pong Diplomacy" occurrence.

When he was 19, he was on the U.S. Olympic ping pong team, about to compete in China. Do you remember the movie *Forrest Gump*? When Forrest was playing ping pong in the movie, that part of the movie was loosely based on Glen Cowan, I believe.

The night before the big game, Glenn went out partying, with his bad-ass self and his long hippie hair. When morning came, he was late for their team's private bus. So they left without him. He went over to the Chinese team's bus to hitch a ride. When he got on the bus, no one said a word to him. They weren't allowed to. It was strictly forbidden. Actually, Fran told me, one guy did. His name is Zhuang Zedong. He got out of his seat, walked to the front of the bus where Glenn was and got an interpreter so they could talk to each other.

Zhuang even gave Glenn a silk tapestry of China's Huangshan mountains. I've seen it, it's beautiful. It hung in Fran's dining room.

The next day, Glenn scoured the city to find a gift for Zhuang. He did: identical T-shirts – one for Zhuang and a matching one for himself. The T-shirt quoted The Beatles' song, "Let it Be."

The Chinese press got a picture of that; the photo made it all the way to their leader at the time, Chairman Mao. Fran said she figured this was looking bad for the Chinese, behaving the way they were. Hell, if two strangers could get along, maybe there's something to this. She also said Chairman Mao must have known he'd look majorly all in the wrong if he'd stuck to protocol in killing Zhuang for being disobedient, talking to an American. He lifted the ban against America and invited President Nixon over for a beer. Okay, maybe not a beer... but I'm sure it was some kind of liquid refreshment.

Star Struck in LaLa Land

Those six months in California, I really hated calling home, because every time Randy answered, he was out having fun without me. There's no other way I could say that. But he was getting everything in order for us to move to the west.

Meanwhile, I was having fun engaging in my own personal Star Search.

My first star sighting in Hollywood was at a Carl's Jr. fast-food restaurant at the corner of La Brea Avenue and Santa Monica Boulevard. It's not there anymore; I think there's apartments there now. I was standing in line when a huge black SUV pulled up. Out popped Lorenzo Lamas. It was lunchtime but he wasn't there to eat; it was cuter than that. He was taking his kids to the restroom. I didn't even know he had kids! The kids looked just past the toddler stage, but not by much. Lorenzo was carrying one of them like a sack of potatoes – just hanging there in his arms with no complaint – and walking the other. I was amazed at how comfortable they all looked and what a regular guy he seemed. Geek runs in my blood and I didn't want to geek out on a regular dude. I got the hell out of there in a hurry, so I wouldn't make a fool of myself.

I also saw that chick from *Scream*, Neve Campbell. We were at the Beverly Wilshire bar named the CUT. It was around 4 p.m. on a rare cool-and-grey weather day. Randy and I were sitting at the bar when I turned around and saw Neve sitting at the round tables behind us. She was fucking beautiful, wearing a soft white button-down blouse with silky-looking black slacks that flared out at the bottom. Black heels, and a cigarette in her right hand, just dangling in midair, leaning against an armrest... giving off the impreison she didn't care one bit if you were looking at her. To me, she looked the epitome of Hollywood. I couldn't stop looking at her. So as to not geek out on her, I only spied on her from behind Randy's shoulder.

I'll tell you who doesn't give a shit what anyone thinks, and that's Randy.

"Look who's over there," I told him, doing my best to inconspicuously point out Miss Campbell.

He turned around really slowly, like I asked him to. Then he looked back at me and said, "She's just like us, Darren."

That helped me snap out of my starstruck-itis.

I do have one small regret while I was in California. Yes, it involves a TV star – well, a superstar to me. My classmates and I had just come out of class at the Second City Comedy School on Hollywood Boulevard around 8 p.m. We went to a local comedy club down the street and who's across the bar? George Wendt, who played Norm on *Cheers*.

We all got excited and I said, "I wanna yell out 'Hey, Norm!'"

My fellow comedians jumped on me and said, "No. Famous actors don't like it when touristy people come at them."

I said, "So what? I'll buy him a beer."

"I don't know about that, Darren," they all said.

I went to the bar and asked the bartender if that was who I thought it was.

It was, but I ended up not buying him a beer.

Damn, I wish I'd never listened to them! I totally wanted to buy Norm a beer. Oops! I mean *George*. Maybe they were right.

Okay, here's a fun sighting that could have landed Randy and me in jail. Randy and I were driving one Saturday morning and Andrew Dice Clay, my brother Ricky's favorite comedian, drove by in a sweet, big-ass red truck. He drove into a Beverly Hills neighborhood off Santa Monica Boulevard. We were heading west, he was going east. We did an immediate U-turn, and I think he saw us. He pulled up to this mansion. It was a light green – a green you don't ask Pittsburgh Paint to make very often.

We weren't *stalking* him, in the truest sense of the word, but when he got out of his truck, he did scurry to his front door in kind of a rush. Sorry, Dice, if we scared you! We were just fanning out.

Because I worked for Fran, and she worked at the Hollywood Improv, I got to meet a bunch of comedian stars. Kevin Nealon seemed nice enough. I found it interesting that he used to be a bartender for the Improv, yet he never drank. Sarah Silverman seemed to prefer smoking her cigarette to talking to me. I wish I'd offered her a joint to lighten the moment. But, that moment's gone.

But the nicest comedian by far was Lewis Black. I met him in the Improv dining room. It was around 4 in the afternoon, while I was waiting for Fran to finish up. The restaurant was closed, so not many people were still around. I asked him if he had any advice for an aspiring entertainer.

He paused for a second, took a breath and said, "Just be yourself. Don't ever try to be anyone else but yourself. Then be the best you can be."

I could swear we were doing an Army commercial!

I extended my hand in thanks, and he shook it. Then Fran walked in, and of course they knew each other. They exchanged greetings, then Fran and I left. I hadn't expected Lewis to be so giving. That was a really cool moment for me.

One last sighting. I was at the weed store – it's legal here. I rolled up into the small back parking lot, to this dispensary about 200 feet across from Barney's Beanery (best restaurant in L.A. – go visit that place! They've got a table with Janis Joplin's name carved in it hung from the ceiling). There's a brand-new light-brown two-tone Rolls Royce parked crooked in the parking lot. It pissed me off a little. Why can't these "richies" park like normal people instead of being inconsiderate and taking up more than one parking space?

I walked into the store from the back door; there were only four other people in there. Two staff members behind the counter and two customers. One looked familiar. About five inches taller than me, he was bald, fit and wearing tight, salmon-colored long shorts and a tight striped tank top. He looked like Mike Tyson. But from where I stood, I couldn't see his whole face.

Plus, I said to myself, there's no way in hell this is Mike Tyson.

As if he could hear my thoughts, he turned his head to the right as he talked to the cashier. And there it was, his distinctive facial tattoo.

I froze. My jaw dropped and I couldn't lift it up. I've been wanting to run into a rich famous person – to ask for help for a come up, even could I sing for you, tell me what'cha think, that kind of thing. This could have been the rich famous person… but that wasn't going to happen. I couldn't move, let alone speak!

I knew the cashiers were watching me, too, but none of us said a word. I glanced over at the cashier to get her to confirm who the customer was. Wearing a huge grin, she nodded.

He stayed for a minute more, shook hands with the cashier he was talking to, then left.

After the door closed behind him, the girl behind the counter said, "Darren, you can close your mouth now."

We all burst out laughing. They said he comes in occasionally.

The very next morning, on a talk show, there he was again, in the same outfit (the segment must have been recorded the day before, unless he's just like me and isn't afraid to wear an outfit twice in a row), talking about giving up weed for good.

I'll say it again: Holy Shit! Welcome to Hollywood.

Close Encounters of the Crack Kind

This may be the last time I write about being on crack cocaine. I don't like it, and I don't like giving it this much attention. Once, while on that shit, I swear I saw an alien ghost thingy lean in on me.

I went all Howard Hughes nutty on myself. I had barricaded myself in my bedroom with a big bag of dope. Randy was still in Florida; we hadn't switched yet. I was on my fourth hit, flying high, with my mattress up against the door so no one could bust in on me.

After an exhale, my head buzzed loudly. When I looked toward the door, a skinny, alien-looking creature appeared – like the space guys from the Ron Howard film, *Cocoon*. Bright white, it stood about three and a half feet tall, bald, with a big, lightbulb-shaped head and big black, slightly slanted oval eyes. It was like he was standing on one side of the door, then he leaned through and peeked around the mattress.

When we made eye contact, he looked shocked that I could see him – and you better fucking believe I was close to shittin' my pants! Then he leaned back and was gone.

I put the pipe down after that. I wondered if the drug was some kind of porthole to another dimension. I'll never know for sure, but that was that!

Time to Make the Switch

I moved back to Florida, and Randy started his new life in Hollywood. Right around then he also started being my manager and agent. He got me on the work crew of the Barbara B. Mann Performing Arts Hall Theatre, in Fort Myers. He figured if I was going to be putting on plays, I might as well go work for the biggest one in the area.

I was amongst 20 or 30 hardy adults who seemed to love working there, too. We were in charge of everything going on backstage. We handled the unloading and loading of the semi trucks before each stage production. Our "uniforms" seemed to always be black T-shirts from the previous production, and blue jeans and sneakers. Some show loads were small and the work was easy; then there were the large productions – ones that gave everybody a woody.

We got to work on *The Lion King*. I won't give away any secrets of their backstage theatrics, but I will say this: The math that went along with the mechanics of the set blew my mind! Their puppetry was incredibly sturdy and built to last. There were at least three semi trucks of sets and props and rigging that needed to be unloaded, but I didn't care. I was in heaven! I think they paid for craft services, too – an all-you-can-eat lunch buffet. Anything you wanted, from a bowl of cereal to cheeseburgers; fruit was always included, too.

I worked there for six months before I headed back to LA. for good. Funny, though, the crack seemed to loosen its grip a bit, so as not to fuck with my work. I did show up hung over once, but never again. I really didn't want to ruin my relationship with the stage. I Love Her. I loved everyone I worked with, too. I talked to every worker I could, asking each one what seemed like a million questions. They answered every one lovingly. I crawled all over that stage – with permission, of course. I was even taken to the highest point in the theatre, where the vertical curtains went up when the show opened. At the top there's a brick wall at the end. There were signatures on it. So I signed Dagwood – my stage name. Let me tell you how I came about my stage name.

About six years before we left for L.A., I'd been waiting tables at The Mill Restaurant in Fort Myers. On my first day on the job, I handed in my first order to our chef, Chef Doug.

He looked at my lunch order with my name clearly visible on it, then hollered out, "Who's Dagwood?!"

We all laughed, but I got goose bumps all over, because I'd been twirling stage names around in my head. I wasn't wanting to go on stage as Darren Numer, for fear of being discovered as a criminal derelict.

Thanks, Chef 'Doug E. Fresh' (that was my nickname for him, because he was a big white dude who love rap music, like me), you helped me get closer to the stage!

Now back to Barbara B. Mann Hall Theatre. Here's another fun fact. The woman who owned that theatre – the very woman herself, Barbara B. Mann – lived right around the block from us and she came to our home for our first play. I was passing out invitations on my street when I happened to knock on Barbara's son's front door.

He said, "Why don't you go invite my mom to this? She likes plays." Then he said her name and I could have passed out! The woman was famous. Hell, her husband built the biggest theatre in our town for her!

I can't take credit for charming her into our home. My pretty little redhead Lucy from the Orpheus Theatre

Group did it. Barbara melted for her when we knocked on her door. She didn't care for me. But she did pull up in our driveway – in the biggest brand-new gold Cadillac – to come watch our play in our living room on Burtwood Drive with about 15 other invited guests.

My last six months in Florida went fast. Thank God. I was sick of the people I was hanging with – mostly drug addicts or dealers. And I had become an embarrassment to my so-called "true friends." Too bad, so sad.

My last working day at the theatre was a warm one; the stage manager wished me Love and luck, and said, "Hurry up and bring us back a play," because I had told everyone I was a playwright, of course!

They all wished me well… and I was on my way. Or I should have been.

But a week before I moved back to California, I was without a car. Randy's car had already been shipped and we had no clue how to get me back there. Then, out of nowhere, a blessing came via my friend Charrie (who had been my neighbor when I was in St. Petersburg building that garage and learning to fly). She called me and said a friend of hers out west needed someone to drive her new Cadillac from Fort Myers, Florida, to L.A. What were the odds?!

So, as the song goes, "we loaded up the truck and we moved…" well, you know the rest.

Swimmin' Pools... *Movie Stars*

We actually did move to Beverly Hills, but not like the Clampetts. For one thing, we didn't have $60 million. And we certainly didn't have Mr. Drysdale finding us a mansion right next door to his. In fact, when we first arrived, we were homeless for a day. Something went wrong with the guys delivering our house stuff, and they were going to be three days late. I dropped off the Cadillac in the Valley. Randy met me there. It was around 6 p.m. and we were getting antsy for a place to live.

Randy had found us a small place, and had put a $500 deposit down on it. On a scale of one to 10, it was a four. The landlord lie about the housing conditions in her brochure. When the old blonde Hungarian landlord pulled out the contract to sign, she pointed out where it said in the contract the apartment was spotless and clean.

It wasn't. Cracks in the walls, uneven floors and much more.

Just as Randy was about to sign, I reached out and took the pen out of his hand.

I said, "Can we have a day to think about it?"

"Sure," she said, "but no more than two days. I have other people looking at the place."

We stayed at the Westin for the night, because they allowed dogs.

The next morning, we drove all over the city looking for a home. We picked up a newspaper and one of the first available places was a room for rent in the poor side of

Beverly Hills. Well, there really isn't a poor side, but if there was, this was it. The landlord showed us a one-room apartment no bigger than a fancy bathroom in one of those hoity-toity restaurants – maybe even smaller. Then he took us to the top of the building and showed us the salt water swimming pool on the roof. We were 11 floors up and the pool and the panoramic view were amazing! The best part was it was pet friendly.

The movers came the following day, shoved all our stuff in that closet-sized embarrassment of an apartment and left.

I grabbed Randy and began to cry, terrified we had made a huge mistake.

He said, "God didn't bring us all the way out here just to dump us off. It's gonna be alright."

He was right. We began to make friends right away and, because we took forever getting back to that first landlord, she canceled our contract and gave us back our deposit. Thank you, Jesus.

We stayed four years in that hovel, almost never inviting anyone over. It was on the first floor, in the very back of the building. The back entrance of the building was right beside our own back door. And it would slam every time someone went in or out. *Every fucking time.* Lucky us.

Clearing Hurdles with National Velvet

But it was time to get to work. Randy and I had come to Hollywood to put on a play – and that's what we began to do. Our stage adaptation of *National Velvet* was finished and the rights and permissions had been granted.

Because I was working with Fran at the Improv, she said we could put the play on in their small back room. The next step was casting.

Through this process, I would make a new lifelong friend. Her name is Tara and she lives in the Valley with her husband and two kids. She was a receptionist at one of these doctor's offices I would take Fran to so often.

As I sat in the waiting room, I told Tara about a play I was going to put on.

She said, "My daughter might like to be in it."

We set up an audition meeting under a big tree in the front yard of Beverly Hills School, down the road from where we lived (that tree's not there anymore, darn).

When Tara showed up, her little girl wasn't there, but her younger son was. He liked what he heard, and got on board.

I had this strong desire to confess to Tara about my drug addiction. I felt if she was going to let me direct her 11-year-old son, I had to come clean about myself.

She told me, "Thank you for being honest about yourself. We all make mistakes."

The play was coming together like a breeze. The auditions went well; rehearsals were fun. But in the middle of rehearsals, our male lead bailed out. So I took over the part and we finished rehearsals, then it was on to our eight-week show.

At the end of the eight-week run, I canceled the play.

It had finally dawned on me the story of *National Velvet* was about a horse race that potentially raises the risk of horses breaking their legs when jumping obstacle fences on the course – making them more likely to have to be put down (killed). Also the horses are harmed by people riding on them and getting repeatedly smacked on the ass with a stick. All this just so people can get their rocks off on that *I'm-better-than-you* feeling.

I don't like that behavior and I decided I'm not going to glorify it.

End of show.

An Inevitable End

While we still lived in Beverly Hills my boss, Fran, passed away. I think she was 96 years old. She died in the hospital and, because I wasn't family, I wasn't allowed to visit her. This bothered me for a while, but I realized it was more important that her family – her only surviving son – be with her in her last days, not me. They weren't as close as she and her son Glenn had been. But that never stopped her from buying pistachio ice cream and stopping by Marie Calender's, picking him up a lemon-meringue pie for the weekend, when he and his wife and her two granddaughters would visit. She really did Love her family a lot; she bragged about them all the time.

Oh my goodness. I almost forgot about the funniest moment I had with Fran. This took place shortly after she was let go as a secretary at the Improv. It was rumored she got caught stealing three cases of Sweet-n-Low packets. She hid them under her skirt. Then tried to say she was wearing the latest style. They almost believed her, but as soon as she ended that statement, one of the boxes fell out from between her legs. The jig was up. She was fired.

Nah! I'm just kidding.

She was getting up there in age and inevitably, well you know. Tick-tock, all clocks stop.

So she was forced into retirement with pay. I think I remember her telling me that. Anyhow, to the funny story.

She was bored one morning, and I asked her, "When was the last time you walked on the beach?"

Fran paused a long time. "I don't remember," she said at last.

So off we went immediately to the ocean.

As we arrived, I saw what looked to be kind of a clear path to the water. Maybe 20 people on the beach. It was pretty open space. So we marched onward. Now to get to the smooth flat sand, you had to climb down a three-foot ramp of softball-size rocks. I took Fran's hand and wrapped it around my arm. She started to wobble to the right, I was wobbling to the left. I stopped wobbling and leaned into her to hold her firmer. But instead, she was falling down and pulling me down with her – and fast!

Within one second, time slowed down in my life. I somehow managed to grab hold of her. I pulled her body up against mine really tight with one arm. I then pressed her head against my chest in a locked down position. Then we tumbled down the bumpy hill like an unwanted rolling pin, shoes flying to all four corners of the earth. We rotated at least three times. When we finally stopped, and arrived to the finish line of humility, I was on my back; she was lying on top of me. All that came to me right after that was that iconic movie scene of a young couple embracing on the sandy beach as the water splashed over them. But the only thing hurled our way was concern from other beach-goers. *Oh my God.* They all witnessed it.

"Are you guys okay?!" they hollered out. I looked at Fran.

Without a word from me, she said, "I'm okay."

I nodded my head yes in reply to their question then together we burst out laughing. We stayed there on the ground laughing for almost a minute. We were a sight to behold. No lie. We were embarrassed, but we Loved every moment of it.

Then that day came.

Fran's funeral was hard for me to deal with because I had lost a best friend, not just a boss. The reception was beautiful. It was held at the Improv. Tons of people showed up. I knew hardly any of them, but to see well over 200 people show up in tribute to this great woman was incredible. I on purpose do not think of her, I really miss my friend too much. Rest in peace, Fran.

Shortly after Fran's passing away, I had to get a job.

One of Fran's best friends, Lynette (who used to assist with managing the Beach Boys), told me, "Darren I hear you singing every so often. Why don't you sing at nursing homes? You can make money doing that."

I had no idea such a job existed!

I put a song list together – just in case I got hired right away.

My first audition was at the Beverly Hills Sunrise nursing home. For my audition, I sang Louis Armstrong's "Wonderful World."

When it came time to negotiate a fee, the activities director who interviewed me said, "We offer $100 to those who are beginners and $125 to those who are skilled."

I said, "I'm skilled. I'll take $125."

She then said those dreaded words: "Don't call us, we'll call you."

I continued to bomb auditions for like six months, but then finally it happened. I learned to tell the activities directors, when asked how much I charge, "I will work with your budget."

That's how you get a gig in my profession.

To my dear Lynette: Thank you for steering my course in the right direction.

The heroin-overdose death of one of our young neighbors signaled it was time for us to leave Beverly Hills. While she was in rehab, a friend threw a packet of heroin over the wall; it turned out to be a bad batch. She was only 19.

We disappeared like a fart in the wind, not telling anyone we were moving. I loaded up my minivan at 3 in the morning two nights straight and we moved into a little house at the end of a dead-end street – which was actually Randy's secret wish.

We were on waterfront property if you can call it that. It was actually a large cement creek that runs behind our street. We moved into a white two-bedroom house with a nice backyard and a spa. I believe we were the only white people on that street; it was mostly Hispanic and black people. I felt perfectly at home. Randy, on the other hand, felt a bit apprehensive. He did lead a sheltered life... at least, I think that's what they call it.

I Was Gross to be Around

I was gross to be around. For almost two decades this drug, crack cocaine, would hold me up for days at a dealer's house or isolated in a motel, trying to jerk off my limp dick. Then its aftermath would ground me for three days in bed, huddled in shame, taunting me with fake suicidal thoughts.

There was no intervention, no standing in church or jail that woke my senses up to get sober of crack. A year or two before the drug was removed from me I was getting tired of being on crack. Randy was tired of me lying to him when we were about to go out and light the night up.

He'd ask me, "Darren, are you jonesing to do drugs? Should I take your keys away from you?"

I lied and said, "Nope, but thank you for asking."

Now, like I said, I'm tired, too, so I said to Randy, "Would you like to know the magic word for me to be honest with you?"

Now I swear I could hear small silent pleadings from wherever, hollering, "Don't tell him!"

Randy said, "Yes, what are you talking about?"

I said, "Say 'Lovingly.'"

"What do you mean?"

"When you ask me if I'm jonesing to do dope, if you ask with the word Lovingly in it, I won't lie to you."

As quick as a jack rabbit escaping a lucky-foot factory, Randy asked, "Lovingly, can I have your keys?"

Just like that, my keys were his. That was a good

night.

We all have secret Love buttons. Sometimes we have to reveal them in order to save a life.

(Look up on YouTube "Darren performs at the Special Olympics World Games 2015." At 15 minutes and 5 seconds is the precise moment when the lines I was singing were all too true to my heart. I almost lose it on stage there, true.)

New House, New Neighbors

I made a brand-new friend directly across the street. Barbara and I became friends instantly. She used to be a vice president of a bank, but is now retired and lives with her son. At the time, her father lived with her, too; he was extremely elderly, bedridden and only had about a year to live.

In this new house I am happy to report the drug crack cocaine would finally fall away from me completely. I know this because I messed up once and only once in that house, and I didn't like how I felt. Truthfully, I could feel the drug being taken out of me.

I had a secret prayer to God and that was, "Please let me be able to go out and have a fun time and put on a beer buzz but don't turn me into a zombie anymore. I can't handle it."

I got my wish. Hell, more than that, my Vision from years earlier had run its complete course.

I want to say I don't care whether you believe me, but that wouldn't be true. I do care what you think. I believe it's in all of us that we do really care what other people think. If we didn't care, there'd be no need for newspapers, news channels and the internet. To me, the people who truly don't care what other people think are the ones who are lost. I want to say I pray for those like that, but I'd be lying. I, like my brother Ricky, don't enjoy praying for educated fools.

About a year after we moved in, I was in my living

room when I heard a commotion going on in the street outside. When I looked out, I saw my neighbor's son about to hit another neighbor (who was a little bit off her rocker) with a baseball bat. By now we were pretty good friends with all our neighbors, except for the one who was "off her rocker."

I bolted out, barefoot, across the street to prevent a collision that would have definitely ended bloody.

I pushed the young man back. "She's not worth it, man," I told him.

I stopped the guy from clobbering her and what thanks did I get? Off-Her-Rocker Lady let out her dogs, one of whom came over and bit me in the ass.

One last story about our time in this house.

All around us were kids, mostly in their late teens to early 20s. So that means a bunch of short-tempered mental loudmouths shooting off their wars of silliness.

One time, about eight of them were in the front yard, surrounding two younger girls about to be in a fist fight. I could tell because all the guys had their cell phones out recording it.

I put down my Chardonnay big gulp, then prayed to God really quick as to how to defuse this situation.

I stepped outside my door, contemplating turning on the garden hose and squirting everyone down. Instead, I received a vision of Julie Andrews spinning on top of that hill in *The Sound of Music*.

So, in the middle of my front yard, I lifted my arms in the air and started twirling and singing, "The hills are alive with the sound of music!"

As I was twirling around with my arms in the air, singing, I realized this wasn't exactly going to work out to defuse things. Half the crowd did notice me and chuckled a little, but the two girls were getting louder and hurling the N-word back and forth at each other. They were both black, as was everyone else around them.

They kept screaming at each other, "[N-word],

who do you think you are?!"

Then I quickly asked upstairs to my Pops if I can go for it, stop this fight in a whole daring other way.

I got a "Yup" in reply – and I've learned you *don't* disregard a "Yup" from the Big Guy!

I got between the two of them and started screaming, not making eye contact with either of them.

I shouted, "I'm the baddest Nigga ever! Ever! You feel me! Nigga! The baddest mutha-fuckin' Nigga ever! You feel me mutha fuck!?"

Aaand that did it.

All the attention was on me now. *All* of it. I broke out laughing, to ease the tension. I could see everyone begin to relax; it was amazing. Then I toke both the girls' hands and made them shake. I think they even hugged. We all didn't laugh as hard as I wish we had. However a war that was about to erupt – a small but powerful one – ended. I Loved how the arts, music & laughter saved the day.

Deaths in the Family...
and Our Newest Addition

Before we moved into our wonderful new neighborhood on the edge of Inglewood, two deaths in my family left me shattered. The first I saw coming a year ahead of time, after I went home to visit my family in Pittsburgh.

My brother Ricky had become extremely skinny and had adopted a terrible habit of falling down on a regular basis. Before I left Pittsburgh, I told Lisa and Billy they needed to keep an eye on Ricky; his legs were giving out on him and he didn't look like he was doing too well.

Ricky had been the wild child in our family. My stories I've shared pale in comparison to my brother Ricky's life. While I was only homeless a few times, he was homeless constantly. If it hadn't been for Mummy, Ricky would have been 100% homeless. Mummy was smart enough to put herself through a government program, which provided her a place to live in an apartment building that housed the mentally ill and troubled citizens. When she thought no one was looking, Mummy would sneak Ricky up to her eighth-floor apartment. But the truth is, they were always looking and never said a word.

Many years earlier, Ricky was given the responsibility to babysit Lisa's three young boys. Instead of babysitting, he went around the corner of the house and banged some chick in a church – at least that's what he told me. I could never be sure of the truth of any of his stories. He once told me he squashed a gerbil to death with his bare hands. Why he would tell me these ridiculous tales, I don't know.

One time, after a visit to Pittsburgh, Ricky, Billy and I went walking across the Smithfield Street Bridge late one night. We were heading somewhere, I didn't care where; I was just happy to be with 'em both.

Ricky said, "Watch this."

He climbed over the railing of the bridge and climbed down about three feet more and hung over the bridge with his feet dangling. This was the scariest thing I've ever witnessed in my life.

It became even scarier when Ricky looked up into my eyes and said, "Brother, grab my hands. I'm slipping."

I grabbed one hand, Billy grabbed the other and we pulled him up to safety. But, shit, that was scary! It was at least a 200-foot drop into the river.

Years later Billy asked, "Do you know why Ricky did that?"

I didn't.

"It's because he's jealous of you, Darren. He's always been jealous of you," he said. "Do you remember right before he climbed over the bridge, Darren? You did a cart-wheel and a backflip."

"Yes, I remember that," I replied. I remembered exactly *why* I did it, too. I was ecstatic about walking across a bridge with my brothers for the first time ever in my life. I wanted to show them what I had learned in my childhood, in all those different foster homes I lived in, but had never had the chance.

Billy told me, "Well, he was trying to outdo you, and that's why he climbed over the railing."

I didn't see it as jealousy at all. I never got that feeling from him, not once.

But yes, Ricky was growing intensely skinny and I needed to emphasize to Lisa and Billy – because they both still lived in Pittsburgh – that they *really* needed to keep an eye on him. For the most part, they never really welcomed Ricky into their lives as adults.

Ricky was also notorious for not making himself

noticed and they were busy raising their own families, I fully understand that.

About a year later, the phone call came, informing me Ricky was in the hospital and I should come home to see him. The cancer had spread throughout his body and wasn't giving up.

Randy and I flew up and headed straight for Allegheny General Hospital. I turned the corner into his room and stared at him quietly as he lay sleeping. His body had become unrecognizable. My beautiful brother was leaving this world and I couldn't do anything to stop it. I wanted him to wake up and immediately challenge me to an arm wrestling contest. I needed to see him pound on his chest and ask, "Do you feel me?"

But those days were all over. In his hospital room, there were cans of Ensure drinks for him to nourish his body. I have nothing against Ensure, but whenever I saw people drinking it in the past, it was usually a friend with AIDS, dying. I began crying uncontrollably and became scared I was going to wake my brother up with these sobs and these tears falling way too fast.

I left his room, walked to the end of the hallway and let the tears fall on the floor, just as I'm doing right now.

In less than six months, Ricky was gone. I didn't go back to Pittsburgh. There was no funeral service. I imagine the local pubs he patronized, the 222, the Key West and the Young Men's Republican Club, all located on the North Side, raised a drink for Ricky the Roofer. Rest in peace, my beautiful brother. Rest in peace.

The second death caught us all by surprise. I was on the back porch with Randy and our across-the-street neighbor, Barbara. We were sitting by the fire pit we had created in the fire grill. My phone rang and the caller ID showed it was my brother Billy.

When I answered, Billy began to tell me his 18-year-old son Jesse had been hit by a train a few hours earlier. He was in the hospital and it didn't look good.

I told him we'd pray for Jesse and hope for the best.

Less than a half an hour later, Billy called me back to say Jesse had passed away. The injuries to his face and chest were more than his young body could take.

It struck me that I didn't know Jesse at all. When I would go back to Pittsburgh to visit my family, I'd try to visit with Billy and his family. But for some reason, that always seemed impossible. I took that to mean that Billy was just too busy to make time for me.

One thing I remember from that night was Barbara walking over to me while I sat on the porch, numb from Billy's news. She hugged me and let me cry. If she said anything to comfort me, I don't remember it.

Randy put me on an airplane to fly home immediately. He joined me a few days later to attend the funeral service.

I had never seen so many young people gather at a funeral in my life. The service was held in a huge cathedral; and not one seat was available. People in the back were standing. I had recently broken my ankle and had to hobble around with a big cast on my foot. I was in the back, sitting in a chair with my crutches. Apparently, my nephew Jesse was an extremely popular football player; his whole school came to the funeral. There's nothing sadder than a bunch of young kids mourning. Rest in peace, my nephew, Jesse. Rest in peace.

I don't want to end this chapter on two sad stories. So let me tell you something good to put a smile on your face; that's how I always love to end my days.

This is how we came to get the newest addition to the family in our new neighborhood. One Sunday morning, while driving to the store to get breakfast, I noticed a woman and her three young children crossing the street, chaperoned by this adorable American Pointer puppy. He was white with brown patches on his face, and he was bouncing all around this Hispanic family as they walked.

At the corner of 81st and Crenshaw Boulevard, I wound my window down and hollered, "Who does that dog belong to?"

The woman yelled back, in her beautiful, silky accent, "I do not know, but he needs a home!"

I drove one block ahead and got out of my minivan. I waited for the family and that bouncy little dog to come into view, which they did in three seconds. Then I opened my passenger door, whistled loudly and called out, "Come here, boy! Come here!"

He came running and jumped right into my arms.

About 30 feet away, the woman and her children were cheering and clapping. I looked over and gave them a big wave and blew them a kiss, indicating I was thankful we'd met. I drove around the block once more to honk my horn at them, saying another thank you. They had the biggest smiles on their face – which I'm sure were about as big as mine.

I started for home, staring at this dog that was now officially in our life. I called Randy, but I didn't mention anything about the dog. I just asked, "Are you up?" When he said yes, I said, "Okay, I'll be home in like two seconds."

On my way home I drove by Barbara's house (she moved to her boyfriend's home around the same time we moved to our new home – a few blocks down the road, ironically) to show off our jumpy new dog. He leapt out the window as I was talking to Barbara, but he didn't go far. And he came when I called him back. Then I rolled my windows up higher, so he couldn't jump out again.

Barbara said she thought he must belong to someone, because he was too clean to have been a street dog.

As I pulled up to our house, my neighbor Eric's son, Eric Jr., approached.

"My father just had a heart attack! Can you take me to the hospital to visit him?"

In a slight panic, I said, "Definitely. Just give me five minutes."

I ran inside. "Hey, Randy, look at that dog outside; do you like how he looks?"

"He's beautiful. And I had a feeling you found a dog. I heard it in your voice."

"Well you're going to have to babysit for a few hours," I said. "Eric across the street had a heart attack and I have to take his son to the hospital to see him."

Everything turned out okay for Eric. But I couldn't help feeling a little guilty, and partially responsible, because the night before I'd fed him stuffed pork chops. And then he had that heart attack around 1 a.m. He was released from the hospital two days later with a strict diet plan. No more stuffed pork chops!

By the time I got home from the hospital, Randy was already in love with the puppy. Our next step was to find out if he belonged to anyone, or if we could keep him... and then come up with a name for him. It turned out his original name was Zeppelin.

His previous owners, who lived two hours north, apparently dumped him in South L.A. At first we were dumbfounded that someone would do a thing like that to such a beautiful creature, but we soon learned he was somewhat of a handful.

Whenever we left, he wanted to come find us. He was exhibiting signs of separation anxiety. In his first six months with us, that determined pup broke four windows in the house to escape. In doing so, he also busted out the screens – all of which had to be repaired. How he didn't get cut in all his broken-window escapes is still a mystery to us.

But his mischief wasn't limited to escaping. One day, he got hold of a container of blue paint I'd left on the dining-room table. That blue paint went everywhere! The dining room, the living room, kitchen, both bedrooms. There's even speckles of blue paint on the ceiling. Don't ask me how it got there!

He's chewed up two of my tennis shoes and one of Randy's dress shoes. One cool morning, he broke the windshield in my van while barking uncontrollably. That happened in our first week of ownership. However, our poor little Houdini pooch found out the hard way his runaway excursions weren't all fun and games. Three dogs around the corner attacked him when he went onto their property to play. Heroically, Eric from across the street heard the commotion and rescued him. Our little escape artist was badly injured in the attack, including puncture wounds in his legs from those other dogs' sharp teeth.

He still hasn't learned his lesson about escaping, but he is big and strong now – he's definitely not a puppy anymore. We're absolutely in love with him, as is Jack Russell, our other dog. But I think the best part is he doesn't sit on the dining-room table anymore… at least, not when we're around to stop him.

What did we name him? We wanted to name him for the location where I'd found him.

But 81st would have been a silly name for a dog. So Randy named him Crenshaw!

Many, Many Mamas

I've acquired a lot of Mamas over the years and claimed them as my own. I'm going to give out humongous "I Love You"s and "Thank You"s to all the mums I adopted through every place I've lived. Mums in restaurants. Mums at the corner store. Mums in my old neighborhoods. You're all my Mums and I Love you with all my heart. Thank you for taking such good care of me. This book is dedicated to all my Mummys. Foster ones, too.

XOXOXO

Mama Gloria was one of my first adopted mamas; she worked at the Silver Spoon in L.A. She allowed me to call her Mama the first day we met. She's like Flo, on that '70s TV show, *Alice*. She doesn't put up with anybody's bullshit. I met her in my first few weeks of being in Los Angeles and she was kind enough to introduce me to my first Hollywood star, Robert Forster. He was in the movie *Jackie Brown*, directed by Quentin Tarantino. The guy was a true gentleman. I almost cried in front of him, but I didn't. Still, I don't think he would have cared if I did, he just seemed to have a cool heart. But I'll be a tool and be totally honest. For the next few months I would go back to have lunch, to be taken care of by Mama Gloria... aaand yeah, hope to get a peek at him one more time.

I'm still friends with Mama Gloria and her brother Kenny, and will be for life. She doesn't live in L.A. anymore; she had to move to go be near her family. And the restaurant she worked at has transformed into one of those chic seafood restaurants.

Another mama I don't see often anymore (because I live on the other side of town now) owns Irv's Burgers on Santa Monica Boulevard. It's a local landmark. Her kids, who work in the burger joint with her, are Sonia Hong and Sean. They'd serve their burgers on paper plates, with an added special cartoon character of yourself or a little message written on your plate in crayon just to make your day a bit more special. Go visit them if you get the chance. Ask for Mama. You're going to fall in love with her, just like I did.

My newest Mama is named Professor Mama, 'cause she's sweet and I have a crush on her, and I tap with her and her daughter Cathie Nicholas. She is the granddaughter of the famous duo tap dancers, the Nicholas Brothers. Her daughter is our tap teacher, nicknamed Professor. I've been tapping for over a year now, and I Love my tap family. I ain't never gonna quit.

I Love it! Shuffle! Shuffle! Tap! Tap! Tap!

Another amazing thing that happened in this tap class besides making beautiful new life friends was when a woman named Jan asked if I'd like to join the Crenshaw Rotary Club. I hadn't a clue what a Rotarian was. So I joined, only to find out we're a group of people who seek out those in need, whether it's giving dictionaries to under-privileged youth or providing for a veteran in need of a Thanksgiving meal. I Love my Rotarian brothers and sisters everywhere. Especially my Crenshaw posse!

Mama Nancy? I've been saving her for last. She is a foster mother, a biological mother and an adoptive mother. Her family has the most talented artists in it. Because I can't remember all her children's names, I will just mention hers. I'm sure the family understands. I've been writing and directing small plays for a number of years now. Mama and her family would always be actors in my shorts skits. In the "Spark of Love" toy-drive show we staged in 2017 at the Pig 'N Whistle, Mama Nancy told her story of growing up and her love for foster children. Since I've known her, she's become a grandmother and is still kicking butt. I am honored and blessed to know her and her beautiful family. I Love you all.

A Few Final Random Revelations

In these last 10 days, I wrote down notes about things I wanted to say, but wasn't thinking of earlier.

Here is my reasoning as to why I feel being homeless is the toughest job in the world.

The job of a homeless person is 24/7 all years long, and commands little respect, if any at all. And if you think the homeless are just being lazy, go back to school, your ignorance is showing.

You are everyone you Love.

This year (2017) was our 10th anniversary Spark of Love show. Mike Giangreco, stage manager of the gracious and historic restaurant Pig 'N Whistle on Hollywood Boulevard, offered his stage to us again in the back room. We thank Mike and the Los Angeles firemen who come with their fire trucks to pick up the toys donated by the audience for the foster children for the upcoming holiday season. Thank you, ABC-7 Teresa and Ruth, for helping us get started 10 years ago with this rewarding project.

I just learned that when the opposing team hits a home run at a Dodgers game, the Dodgers' fans throw the ball back into the field as if it's a gross, disgusting thing. That's not right. It's not good manners. Behave yourself. Please don't act like a fool.

Imagine you're in the stadium and the grandmother of the guy on the other team who just hit a homerun is sitting next to you. You wouldn't want your grandmother to be belittled in that manner. So why would you disrespect someone else's grandmother? Love each other better. It's a good thing and it feels good, too. This behavior sets a bad example for the children of Los Angeles and everywhere around the world. When *we* behave like that, *they* behave like that.

I dropped two babies when I was younger. I never told anyone that. I tried to balance this one little girl on a shopping cart. I thought she was able to hold herself up, only to watch her fall over and bop her head on the floor. I ran into that kid 15 years later and damned if she didn't give me the stink-eye. I swear to God, she didn't like me one bit... I can't imagine why.

The other kid I dropped... well, I'm thinking of keeping that story to myself because I want to keep my relationship with her mother intact. Sorry, Sarah, my bad. You only cried for a second when you fell off the couch and I didn't catch you. You were a tough one. I bet you still are... wink and an embarrassed smile to her mother, Michelle, and dad, Christian.

I'd like to give a special shout out to a special friend, Ron Goldstein. I befriended him when he was the manager of Fred Segal's on Melrose Boulevard here in L.A., down the street from the Improv. The first day we met, we were instant friends. I hung out at his shop a lot while waiting for my Fran to finish up with her work. Then when Randy came to L.A. for the first time, and I had moved back to Florida, Ron opened his home to Randy 'til he got his own place to stay. We Love you, Ron; thank you so much for all the Love you give us.

Back in Fort Myers, Florida, I got to meet a country singer by the name of Mindy McCready, may she rest in peace. I was invited to her mother's house for Christmas dinner. I'd been there a few times before. Her mother was absolutely generous in feeding others, and they were crazy about Jesus, too, nothing wrong with that! I'd never met Mindy before, but this time someone was singing around the corner while I was in the living room. The voice was that of an angel.

It startled me so much (in a good way) that I blurted out, "Who the hell is that?"

In this way-major Christian home, I guess I kind of offended them, but I couldn't help it. Her voice was so beautiful!

Then I met Mindy, and she was as beautiful as her voice.

But now the funny part of this story goes like this. I was more friends with her aunt than with anyone else in that family. I confided in her that I was a drug addict, but she gave me nothing but Love and respect. She was even a protector of mine during that evening I got to meet her niece.

We were in the Deep South, you don't get any deeper than Fort Myers. Mindy's aunt came up to me when I first walked into the house. She walked me over to the kitchen, where all the food was laid out, then leaned close and said. "Darren, do you see those three guys out there by the pool? They know you're gay and they might want to do you harm. They're drinking, too, so you may want to stay away from them. But do try the potato salad, it's absolutely delicious."

I ended my relationship with her that evening. I was always curious if she wondered why I did that. Well, this is why: One of the guys she was talking about was her husband. It was clear to me that if her husband would say something like that, then truly her attention needs to be on her husband not me, at all. And yes, the potato salad was awesome.

My dearest special-needs homes, senior facilities and the VA hospital here in L.A. and the Long Beach Transit bus company (which hired me to DJ music for them during holiday parades), I always wanted to sing and DJ for people, and you guys allow me to. Thank you sooo much. You see, one time in my early 20s, I bombed in my church choir and refused to return to the stage out of embarrassment. That went on for a really long time. But that isn't the case anymore. Because of y'all, I don't bomb anymore. Well maybe a little, sometimes... Please know, I Love you all.

I must give an acknowledgement to my assistant while I was directing plays for a couple of years. Her name is Laura Kranz. She is an aspiring actress, and has already appeared multiple times on the star-studded show, "Grey's Anatomy." She was an amazing assistant, and even jumped up on stage as an actress when an actor was in need. We wish you Love and blessings. Can't wait to see you on the big screen.

Now I never did much stand up, you have to have a strong passion for the craft. I'm more of a song-and-dance guy. But I relished encouraging my friend Greg Buckman to do stand up. He is one of our longest L.A. friends. He was our hilarious barkeep at the Beverly Hills Polo Lounge. He's blowin' up. WOW! He would always say to me, "Darren, we're gonna make it in this town." That always made me smile. He never once turned me down when I would ask him to donate his comedy time in many of our benefit productions. Well, Greg and your beautiful wife, thank you for the Love. It's time to fly.

A Challenge of Sorts

I want to throw this challenge out to you, my reader, my friend. Give yourself 90 days and tell your story – from start to finish. I bet you've got something good to say. I just bet you do!

A Final Thought: One Last Tear

When I was finished with my 90-day story, I went back and read it over and over. It didn't feel finished. It felt rushed. Which actually it was, so I waited 10 more days, collected more notes, to put a proper ending to this part of my life story.

My manager explained it to me this way: Writing my story in the amount of time I'd given myself was like baking a cake. After baking it, you can't get right into it immediately; it has to cool.

So I took 10 days to let it cool, and added *One Last Tear*.

Other than in the first part, I didn't talk about my family too much in the book. I assume it reflects how I feel about them. My brother Billy – whose hugs and kisses I miss – and we really never got back together as a family after that day I went out for a pack of smokes. But I Love him with all my heart, and his beautiful last surviving son ... but I have to Love him from a distance only, because that seems to be the way he likes it.

My sister Lisa was a constant knuckle-sandwich gift to me, every single time I would go home to visit – about every three to four years. By the third day of our visit, we'd fight like cats and dogs, which would immediately end the visit, most of the time. But it seemed we were only acting out our childhood fights that we never got to share. She beat me up when I was 16 years old, when I told her I was gay. But, as strange as it sounds, I enjoyed the fights, every one of them. My sister has raised three wonderful young boys, now heading into their 20s, with the world at their feet. Blessings to all my nieces and nephews, and their families to come.

Mummy is lying in a state-run facility in Pittsburgh, Pennsylvania. My beautiful brother Billy set her up there due to the instructions given to him by our brother Ricky on his death bed. She is cared for by Loving nurses and wonderful staff members at Kane Hospital. I want to give a special thanks to all those nurses who feed and cared for Mummy.

She doesn't call me on the phone anymore like she used to when we were younger, asking me what I was wearing. I call her on the phone almost never. I'll admit I've wanted her to have a peace of mind in her head for a long time, no matter the cost. Though I've never said that to a single soul before. I imagine she must have hated living the life she did, having to go through the mental hell every single day. I've got the strangest feeling everyone in Mummy's life thinks this way about her, too – from her brothers and sisters who ditched her when she was young, all the way to the rest of us kids.

Well the cake has cooled down. I'm finished with the icing, and crying. Now the only thing left to do is to put this cake on a serving tray, and share it with you.

I Love you, Randy. I Love you, Dad.

In these past few months' time, while I was working with my editor, Rita M. Reali, on my life story, Mummy passed away at 2:55 p.m. on a Saturday.

My mother-in-law called me from Texas to say, "Sorry for your loss." Believe it or not, we kinda get along nowadays – even with Randy's dad, too. I guess the older we get, the less we stress the small stuff.

That said, I want to share what I shared with my mother in-law over the phone about what Mummy had said to me in my 20s when I asked her why she gave up on us kids.

She told me, "I had to, sweetie. I was losing my mind fast, and I didn't want to harm you, and I surely would have. So I prayed to God one day, when no one was looking, that He would take my children away from me, so you all could have a better life."

I Love you so much, Mummy. Rest in peace.

About the Author

Darren Timothy Numer is an amazing, wonderful, accomplished survivor of life. He was born in the Allegheny County Hospital in Pittsburgh, Pennsylvania, on August 30, 1969. His ability to graduate from decade to decade through life had much to do with his view of the world as a huge bowl of gumballs. Darren never looked at life as something hard to chew on, but rather viewed it in terms of how many big bubbles could he blow. When asked what he hopes his biography can do, he's been known to say, "Let's do the impossible – Love Each Other, Love Each Other, Love Each Other!"

CPSIA information can be obtained
at www.ICGtesting.com
Printed in the USA
BVHW09s1949111018
529907BV00001B/263/P